SOULFUL MILES

Finding Light on Life's Darkest Roads

JENN BETHUNE

Post Hill PRESS

A POST HILL PRESS BOOK
ISBN: 979-8-89565-183-4
ISBN (eBook): 979-8-89565-184-1

Soulful Miles:
Finding Light on Life's Darkest Roads
© 2025 by Jenn Bethune
All Rights Reserved

Cover design by Jim Villaflores

Post Hill Press
New York • Nashville
posthillpress.com

Published in the United States of America
1 2 3 4 5 6 7 8 9 10

Kyle, you are my greatest adventure, my biggest mirror, and my deepest reflection. I love living this beautiful life we have created together.

TABLE OF CONTENTS

INTRODUCTION

Everyone's life, no matter who you are, is filled with struggles. I genuinely believe that life will always be hectic. Balance is all about finding your calm amidst the chaos.

The struggles in life came early to me in the form of an abusive mother whom I haven't spoken to in decades. Born from the beauty of that struggle came my desire to break generational trauma and not continue that same cycle of abuse with my children. All the while, I was healing my inner child.

My story began writing itself many years before that life-changing moment of finding footage of Gabby's missing white van and becoming friends with Nichole, Gabby's mom. My soul was cracked open in an incredibly tragic way a decade prior. However, I had no idea then just how connected and intertwined Gabby's story would be with my heart and soul.

So many things have happened for me on my "highway to happy," and this book has been waiting to be written for a very long time. Every struggle I've grown through in my life has led me to where I am. Along the way, I have learned valuable tools to help find my calm in the chaos happening at that time. By using these simple steps when I need them, I can find clarity in any overwhelming moment, and I want to share them with you.

I want you to be able to manage your big emotions of anxiety, fear, grief, dread, abandonment, and so many other debilitating feelings whenever you need to.

Aside from the cost of this book, everything I recommend and share with you is completely free. It won't cost you a penny to live a life of contentment and joy every single day. I want to be upfront, and I must stress and warn you that it's not going to be easy, but it will absolutely be worth it.

I'm writing this book because I want to be a beacon of light, illuminating the path to your own inner freedom.

(You can follow our journey here on our channel and become part of our family: https://youtube.com/@beingbethunes?si=4ZNul9eZplVS93qf.)

If you want to share with me directly, I would love to hear from you. Have a win you want to share in a safe space? Please tell me! Need to vent in a secure place that won't be public? I'd love to be that for you. Sometimes we all need a place to feel what we need to feel without big emotions attached to it. Please email me (onmyhighwaytohappy@gmail.com) because your voice matters. I want to make sure you feel seen and loved, so please send a note any time.

jenn

P.S. I'm so grateful you're here.
P.P.S. I can't wait to see how far you grow.

HIGHWAY TO HAPPY: GET IN THE DRIVER'S SEAT OF YOUR LIFE BY EMBRACING YOUR OWN EMOTIONS

What's a "highway to happy"?

A "highway to happy" is a visual that I use to help aid my mind in finding balance in my life.

For many years, my days were filled with anxiety, anger, resentment, grief, guilt, shame, frustration, sadness, worry, terror, abandonment, criticism, and frankly any other heavy emotion you can feel.

These emotions ranged from mild to severe, and I had absolutely no idea how to manage any of them. Typically, I took them out on those whom I loved most by yelling and screaming. I had so many emotions happening at once, I was immediately thrust into overwhelm, and all those combustible emotions would explode at once. I imagine the Jenn back then wasn't easy to live with on many occasions.

So, how did that Jenn get here, writing this book about managing emotions? For that, we must go several exits back on my Highway to Happy.

MAY 18, 1987

This highway exit is the one where I exited my mother's womb, taking my first breaths into this world.

My mother was in labor for nearly twenty-eight hours before she had an emergency C-section. From the moment she held me for three long months, I cried and cried and cried—because I had colic. There were many times when my mom told me I should be grateful she didn't murder me as a baby. My mom wasn't really a patient woman.

I guess I should confess that I haven't had a great relationship with my parents. It's not for lack of trying, and I can firmly say that it's for the best. Looking back from where I am now in my life, I have clarity. I see my parents' trauma in how they raised me. My parents' trauma came from my grandparents and the way they raised my parents. These same behaviors have endured for generations without each generation ever realizing it was happening.

For me, it all comes down to choices. We all have them. In every single moment, we have choices to make. We make them based on what we think is best for ourselves in whatever season our current selves are in and how much trauma is unhealed.

Basically, we are all unknowingly doing our best with what we have in every single moment. Maya Angelou once said, "Do the best you can until you know better. Then when you know better, do better." If we're intentional with our growth, we recognize when a repeat trigger of heavy and combustible emotions comes up. If we are on our highway to happy, we dig into our trauma to figure out where these big emotions are coming from. When we see which trauma is causing the trigger, we can identify it; accept that it happened; and grow forward to make healthier choices, essentially releasing the trauma and the heavy emotions that accompany it.

I don't resent any choice that I've made over the course of my life. I understand that I was doing the best I could with the knowledge, awareness, and emotions that I had in that particular moment.

And you are too.

I try to remember hindsight is 20/20. Of course, you can look back on your previous choices and see what you could've done differently. It's okay to recognize it. It's not okay to continue to criticize yourself for it. If that choice comes up again, you'll know the right one to make.

That said, here is my story.

Even though my parents and I no longer speak, I recognize and understand that they made choices based on their own generational trauma, and they had no idea they were doing it.

I was the first grandchild of the family; my grandparents absolutely doted on me. In fact, my Nan (my maternal grandmother) is one of my favorite relatives ever to this day.

From ages one to four, I competed in beauty pageants. Yes, the ones where little girls are dressed in gowns intended for much older girls and fully-made up faces, so they can be judged by complete strangers. These events were very popular in the eighties—as was the hair, and at two years old, my mom was perming mine.

I have always had thin hair, so back then, it was customary to get a perm for added thickness. I remember it took hours and smelled absolutely putrid. I'd have to sit on a hard little wooden stool while my mom would take an hour or two wrapping strands of my hair in perm rods. Then, she doused my whole head with the stinky chemical curling solution as I bent over the kitchen sink. Even though I had a rolled-up lengthwise hand towel as a barrier for my eyes from the pungent perm solution, it still burned them and made them water.

I won a lot of titles. I'll never forget when they announced I was "Little Miss Tampa." It came with a six-foot high trophy, and my mother was beaming from ear to ear.

Even at a young age, I wanted to make my mom happy. If I did the things that she wanted me to do, she would be nice to me. If I did one minuscule thing that was not what she expected, it was hell.

The hell varied throughout the years.

My brother came along when I was five and a half. During my mom's pregnancy, she found out that she was expecting twins. She ended up miscarrying my brother's fraternal twin, and I remember she took that hard. I didn't fully comprehend it back then; I just knew I was sad, so she must be sad too. I've always been able to feel others' emotions. Ever since I can remember, I've had tremendous empathy for every person I've ever met. I couldn't wrap my head around what a miscarriage was until many years later when I had two of my own.

As my brother grew, my mom would always make a joke that he ate his brother because he was so fat. I saw him laugh it off, but I felt his pain. That's just the type of person my mother was; she insulted others to see their embarrassment and feel better about herself.

The truth about our childhood is that my mother was, and still is, a very unhealed person. She's the type of person you must walk on eggshells around because you never know when she's going to be triggered and explode next. It was like living around landmines; you had to be vigilant with every step. Even taking the wrong breath could cause one of her triggers to detonate.

She took a lot out on my dad and my brother as well, but it felt like I got the worst of it. Not only was my mother a gaslighter and a narcissist, but she was also immensely jealous…of me.

From the stories I've heard, as well as my own personal experiences, I genuinely believe from the moment I was born that my mother hated me, and she wasn't afraid to make me feel it.

I'm about to tell you a story that I've heard several times, once even proudly told by my mother herself. Some of the versions varied slightly, but the theme is the same.

When I was an infant, my mother and father lived with one of my uncles at his house for financial reasons. At the time, my uncle was a bachelor who pretty much came and went as he pleased, living his best life, as they say now.

Early one morning around 4 a.m., my uncle was startled awake by my mother shoving a bottle in his chest, demanding though a clenched jaw, "Open this fucking thing now! I'm gonna strangle her!"

My uncle groggily took the bottle, popped the lid right off, exposing the nipple. My mother went to snatch it from him; hearing me screaming at the top of my lungs, he said, "Give me Jennifer. I'll feed her."

She shoved me into his arms and stormed out of the room. My uncle fed me, burped me, and then laid me on his chest, where I fell right to sleep.

For many years, my mother made sure I knew how much of a burden I was to her as an infant. I had colic for the first three months of my life, and she never let me live it down

From the moment I left her womb, I genuinely feel that my mother has seen me as a burden.

My mom's father, my Grampy, never held a baby until me. In fact, he left work and rushed to the hospital as soon as I was born. From the moment that he held me, I was the apple of his eye. My Nan has never hidden her favoritism for me from anyone. Nan has always loved and cared for me so incredibly deeply; she was one of the only people I can ever remember feeling proud of me.

At the age of two, I taught myself to use speed-dial on our landline telephone. The rotary phone was out, and buttons were in! Watch out world!

One afternoon, I remember my mother being utterly impossible; and that's exactly what I told my grandmother after I dialed when she picked up the phone. "Mother is being impossible! Can you please come get me?"

About forty-five minutes later, my Nan and Grampy came pulling up to our trailer in their '70s red Ford Econoline Van with a porthole window in the side lovingly named Ol' Red.

I don't exactly remember what my mother was being impossible about, but I do remember that my Nan was my safe space, and she made me feel seen. She was always there, giving me the love I needed.

When I was ten, we had to rush my brother to the emergency room. I remember that day as if it was yesterday. December 22, 1997. My brother's equilibrium was off, and he couldn't walk straight. He had also been vomiting off and on throughout the day. My parents made the decision to rush all of us off to the hospital.

I recollect sitting in one of those old fiberglass metal leg chairs. I was swinging my feet back and forth as the words came out of the doctor's mouth. "Your son has a brain tumor the size of a baseball on his brainstem."

Oh. This isn't good, I thought. The silence made my stomach sink; you could hear a pin drop.

My brother spent three months in the hospital having various surgeries and procedures, and then he went to rehab. While her sole focus was my brother, I was put on the back burner.

I had just started soccer that year, right before my brother's tumor. My mom never came to one single practice or game. My dad had to work, so my mom could stay at the hospital with my brother. He was able to drop me off at some practices while my friend's parents brought me home.

I felt abandoned and alone. Each Saturday, I'd have a different extended family member or my dad at a game for me. I was appreciative that they took the time to be there. However, I just wish my mom had tried to make it to one.

My brother became her life. She doted on him twenty-four seven, and I just became an annoyance to her. My needs were too much as I entered my teenage years.

Of course, understanding duality now, I see how terrified she must have been. Having already lost his twin, her surviving son now had had a life-threatening tumor. She was scared to her core that she was also going to lose my brother. I get why I was relegated to the back burner, but now, as an adult, I also know it wasn't fair. The duality is accepting it all and realizing we are all doing our best at every moment.

For the better part of two decades, my mother and I haven't had a relationship.

When I was growing up, my mother exemplified narcissism. When I was about twelve, I remember she began drinking heavily. She used alcohol as a tool to drown out her big emotions. She started out with wine coolers and soon dove into hard liquor. Narcissism plus alcohol: this combination was purely toxic.

The biggest problem was she got really, really mean when she drank, but she didn't see it. She thought it was "funny" and told me that I was too sensitive; I was the problem. She would give me the silent treatment for hours until I would come back to her, apologizing for what she said I did. I'd have to beg for her love. If I wanted my mother to give me any type of love, it was on her terms. Meanwhile, I was feeling more and more unloved by her.

I was, relatively speaking, a "well-behaved kid." I was never sent to detention at school because I was terrified of the outcome.

I was expected to never question anything my parents said. I was to do what I was told to do, and anything else was unacceptable, and there would be consequences and shame.

I grew up in a house full of controlling, blaming, shaming, and criticizing. If I did one thing out of line (which was anything above being a model child), I would be reprimanded by my dad. The day would go by, and then my mother would get drunk, sit me down at the kitchen table, and yell at me for several hours about the same incident, really driving her point home. Over and over and over she would say how I messed up and made me feel so ignorant for something as simple as forgetting to do the dishes.

My early teenage years at home were hell. My mom would get drunk every night and fight with everyone in the house. Sometimes, it would turn physical as she would push and hit my dad. In her fits of rage, depending on the offense, she would slap me in the face as punishment. There would even be times she would yank my hair or my ear.

On a few occasions, both my mom and my dad spit in my face with disgust, depending on the offense.

Throughout school, I always had good grades and never really got into trouble. My parents took the authoritarian stance, and it was a "do as I say" mentality, or else.

At sixteen, I had started dating a boy I had known from middle school with whom I reconnected by going into a McDonald's for lunch one day. This particular day was a Saturday, and I had been working for my mom as her shampoo girl. My mom was a hairdresser, and she had me come in on Saturdays to shampoo clients and clean her station for her. I would get paid in tips from the customers I shampooed, and she would also give me a some of her tips for the day for working. I'd usually make around twenty dollars for the whole day.

We never really had a lot of money, and my parents struggled to make ends meet each month, and most of my clothing came from outlet stores or Walmart. I took what I made at the salon to supplement my closet and shop at stores like Ross, where I could find name brands at a lower cost. I think that's when my love of thrifting clothes and savvy clearance shopping truly began.

Because of that fateful day at McDonald's, that guy became my boyfriend. Shortly after, my mom invited him to come live with us and allowed him to sleep with me in my bedroom.

Aside from the usual bullying of high school, I was genuinely enjoying my junior year. I had already lettered as a Thespian, made good grades, and was in the JROTC. My senior year was going to be promising, and I had hopes of moving to New York and making it on Broadway after high school. My drama teacher decided on plays, and I was going to be able to grow as an actor with ample opportunities in the coming year.

In December of 2003, I was in eleventh grade, and I got pregnant at age sixteen.

My mother spent a lot of her time gossiping about teenagers who get pregnant and how their moms were failures. She'd always say "my daughter would never do that to me." In all fairness, when I approached her about birth control, she told me I'd need to find the doctor and make the appointment myself. Then, I could let her know the day, and she would take me.

As a forgetful teenager who didn't really know how to navigate the printed healthcare register (because the internet wasn't readily accessible) and locate a doctor, then make an appointment, I got distracted by other things…obviously, lol.

Knowing my mom's explosive temper, I was absolutely dreading telling her that I was pregnant. I knew that it would be an epic abusive yelling session that would result in her wanting me to have an abortion. I was terrified of her and the abuse that I would come to endure. So, I waited to tell her until I figured things out and made a decision that was right for me.

A day or so after I saw the positive test result, I put my hand on my belly and felt this instant, protective bond. In that moment, I knew I needed to save him, whatever that meant doing.

Well, that meant me not telling my mom until after I was four months along.

The day had come where I could no longer say that I'd "just been eating too much" in response to their questions about my puffy midsection. I knew I needed to let my mother know what was going on.

At the time, my then boyfriend was still living in my bedroom, but spoiler alert: not for much longer.

My boyfriend advocated for me telling my mom by myself because she would take it easier. He didn't have a car at the time, so he arranged for his mom to come and pick him up for the day. We had already told his mom together because we knew she would take it better, and it wouldn't result in any abuse and repercussions.

In truth, he probably just didn't want to be there for it. Being a teenager himself, I imagine he was experiencing his own emotions, and his gut reaction was to flee. He was doing the best he could with what he had in the moment.

In that moment for me though, I was feeling some pretty big abandonment. I was about to face my mother alone. I'd be giving her news that would make her narcissistic self explode on me. But I had run out of time, and the time to tell her was now.

I sheepishly looked around the house for my mother; it was midday, and my dad was at work. I found her tanning herself in a lounge chair on our screened-in pool area. My fingers were twisting in my hands as I walked up to the edge of her beach chair.

"Hey, Mom, so…can I talk to you?" I tried to sound confident asking.

"You're pregnant, aren't you?" she retorted.

Tears began to stream down my face as her face turned to disgust.

She immediately demanded, "How far along are you?"

"S-s-sixteen w-w-weeks…" I stammered.

She knew. She knew what I'd done. If I was this far along, there's no way she would demand I get an abortion, so I wouldn't "ruin my future" as she said in the past. I had waited this long to save this baby. If it was any earlier, because of the cycle of abuse and control my parents had over me, I felt she would have found a way to force me to have an abortion.

"What am I going to tell people? Do you know what people are going to say about me? What is your father going to say?! You're telling him. I'm not telling him."

That day, my dad lost his ever-loving mind and promptly kicked my boyfriend out not long after he got the news.

If I didn't think that life could get worse, I was immensely wrong. Word had obviously gotten out that I was pregnant; luckily it was before social media was a thing, or it would've been more embarrassing for my mother.

Needless to say, my mother was pissed, feeling extremely ashamed, and took every opportunity to express her disdain and disappointment of me. She told me every day how much of a shame it was that I did this to myself. As a minor, I was still on their health insurance, so the medical expenses of my pregnancy would be covered. My mother made sure to mention this financial burden at every chance she could as well.

The first doctor's appointment came, and this was the only time she allowed my boyfriend to come. Once she saw the sonogram, something in her changed. She became protective of the baby, trying to push everyone else away. It was almost as if she had imprinted on him, and he became her sole focus.

My parents had already been controlling and authoritative. I was a child who was molded to behave, always achieve good grades, and follow my parents' orders at all cost. My dad once told me as a young girl, "I don't care if my kids love me; I want them to fear me."

I had been and still was heavily controlled by them from the fear of being in trouble, the ridicule, the long hours of reprimand and disappointment at the kitchen table. With the threat of physical abuse, I learned to fall in line at a very early age.

Standing up for myself by waiting until it was safe to speak of my pregnancy, in fear of being forced to get an abortion, was completely out of character for me. By doing that, their facade of control began to crack within me; I was waking up from years of abuse.

Despite this newfound empowerment, I was still terrified of them. Now I was a petrified and pregnant young girl who felt abandonment at every turn.

My mother began to get controlling, limiting who I talked to on the phone and when I was allowed out of the house. She forbade me from speaking to my baby's father. They told me that they suspected him of stealing one of their laptops, and I wasn't allowed to ever talk to him again.

I didn't have a choice. I obeyed them.

They were paying for my healthcare, I was still a minor, and I was being verbally and physically abused every day. Living with my mother was hell. I didn't have a say in anything; if I disagreed about something related to my baby, there was pure rage from her. If she was triggered by me, yanking my hair was her way of letting me know how full of anger she was.

There was one time I ran away to my boyfriend's apartment when I was around six months pregnant. I couldn't take my mother anymore. I was there for a day when the police came knocking at the door.

We made the mistake of answering it.

Because we had answered the door, and the police saw me, they had to take me back to my parents waiting in the cop car. I was a minor; I didn't have a choice—even after I explained how awful my parents were being to me. The police apologized and told me they wish they didn't have to take me. They advised me to not answer the door next time. If they can't make contact, there's really nothing they can do.

Again, if I thought it had been bad before, it was nothing compared to what began after I was brought home by the police.

I don't remember the trigger, but when I was about eight months pregnant, something set my mother off, and she kicked me out of the house. With the door deadbolted and me in my pajamas, I went across the street to my neighbors and called the police.

When the police came, they immediately went to my mother, who was standing right outside of our gate.

As soon as I saw their faces, I knew. I knew my mother fed them a really great story because she's an expert at swaying people in her favor.

The police officer told me that my mother said, "My daughter isn't well mentally, and she's off of her meds and ran away again. She's done this before."

I was not on meds, I felt pretty stable, and I was locked out of my home by my mother.

Once again, I was made to go back to my parents. My mother had called my dad home from work, and he was expected to arrive any time soon. I was terrified, standing in the kitchen when he walked in fuming. He stormed up to me, pushing me against the stove. He called me a piece of trash before he tilted his head back, cleared his throat, and spit directly in my face.

We stopped speaking shortly after Ethan was born when I was around eighteen. At this point in my life, I found my voice with my mother, and she had a difficult time with that. Her subconscious was realizing that she was losing control of me.

My nineteenth birthday was approaching, and I had graduated from grooming school and became a pet stylist with PetSmart. I had a really great job, a great group of friends, health insurance, and I had just bought my first car.

In healing so much of this inner trauma from around this time period, I know my mom was just doing the best she could with her unhealed trauma. I have let go of the heavy emotions surrounding my mother. It doesn't excuse her parenting choices; it allows me not to carry it any longer.

It was May of 2006, and I had joined Match.com in hopes of dipping into the dating pool. Online dating was beginning to become a popular way to get to know people. Because I was spending my time driving two hours each way to work, then getting back home, sleeping, then repeating, it didn't leave much time to go places and meet people.

I'd gone on a couple of dates, and they were dismal to say the least. Finally, I'd had a guy message me twice. Coming off of a few bad dates, I didn't know if I wanted to endure another. I left the messages unanswered for a few days but then got a third email from him. I had this nudge to give it shot, and I replied back.

I came home at 3 a.m. from our first date, and I told my roommate, "I'm going to marry that man."

And I did.

Two years later to the day of our first date, at the Viva Las Vegas Wedding Chapel, Kyle and I got married.

By the time I was married, and Ethan was five, I refused to have any contact with my mother because of how verbally and mentally abusive she had become. I dreaded her phone calls because they would always end up in her getting triggered if I didn't agree with her. There would be some nights if I didn't answer or tell her I wasn't up for talking, she would call upwards of eighty times in the course of a couple hours until I answered. Everything had to be on her terms, or it would be hell to endure.

She was not only abusive to me but everyone around her. If you didn't do things exactly her way, to the exact expectations she had for you, you received the full wrath of my mother.

It felt like she could shoot daggers right through me with her rage-filled energy. She wanted me to feel her disdain for me. She wanted me to know the pain she was experiencing inside. She wanted to hurt me, so then I would know how she felt. She had to make me feel it, and I felt it very deeply.

As an adult, I always said, "I will never, ever, do this to my kids. Ever." I was adamant in not wanting to be like my mother. I didn't want my kids to ever experience the pain I felt.

But guess what? They did.

Up until the last four years, I didn't know anything about generational trauma or how it affected those around me. There were little things I would do or say that were like my mother. It was unhealthy parenting, and I didn't have a clue that, in fact, I was doing it.

I had all these emotions that I didn't know what they were, where they were coming from, or how to stop them. I would have big sensations of rage and anger, and then I would feel an immense amount of guilt after I exploded.

What I know now is that my generational trauma was showing. It was bleeding throughout my life and seeping into my children's experiences, and I had no idea what was going on.

I've been on my intentional healing journey for a little over four years now. I say intentional because we are always unknowingly doing our best in each moment, trying to heal. When you're intentional, you KNOW that you're doing your best at every moment, trying to heal. It's why I can now forgive my mother for the way I was raised. Just because I didn't have a healthy childhood doesn't mean that my mother didn't help shape me into who I am.

I'd like to be clear: I am forgiving her for myself. I didn't want to carry around the regret of not getting the loving and healthy childhood I deserved anymore. The resentment. The shame. The guilt. The pain. The anger. The sadness. The abandonment.

Those big emotions that she threw onto me that I had been carrying for more than three decades were so heavy and became a burden.

I was sitting with my good friend Delmara one recent summer, camping on a serene and secluded lake. She and I were talking about our mothers. She told me that no matter how her mother raised her, it shaped her into who she was. She became grateful for the life her mother led because it showed my friend that everything is a lesson, and we have a choice in how we grow. Her sharing her healing story about her mother inspired me to finally forgive mine.

As a result of raising me the way she did, I've always felt intense and painful emotions; I grew to be a deeply empathetic person. I genuinely care so much for people and the emotions they're experiencing. I've found freedom in learning to manage my emotions, and I am living in balance most days. My soul wants others to know it's possible to manage their own emotions and find balance in whatever moment of life they are in too.

Through my life of trauma, I am finally able to live happily every day. However, I would like to be clear: I've found that happiness isn't a destination—rather, it's finding balance in your journey.

Life will always be changing and shifting. You'll never live the same moment twice, and control is an illusion. The one thing you have control over in this life are your own choices. Every choice you make is yours and yours alone. The consequences of the choice are also out of your control. However, you get to choose what you say yes and no to. Will there always be factors that affect your choices? Absolutely.

When you're doing your best to live in balance, the choices become easier. Being balanced, you see the whole picture. By living in balance, you're able to have discernment with what feels aligned with you. Discernment allows you to say no to things that don't feel right and yes to the things that do.

To find balance, I had to heal. To heal, I had to listen to myself by what my emotions were trying to tell me. My emotions gave me clues to the trauma I was carrying. Each of the emotions were rooted back to a heavy experience or experiences I had in the past.

The more I listened when each big emotion came boiling over, the more I was able to manage it. If I felt anger rising, I signaled to Kyle or the kids that I needed to move. I would take a quick walk, catch my breath, and ground my feet. Once I came back, I was able to have clarity on the situation, and we could navigate it much easier.

As time went on, the big emotions rising out of control got fewer and fewer. Now, I can take one deep breath in place, and I've got my clarity. I'm able to stay in balance or find it fairly quickly. It wasn't easy work, but the freedom I feel now was absolutely worth it.

I truly believe the school of life is one of the best educations if you allow it to be.

It IS possible to heal—my life is proof. If I can heal, you can heal too. Use your hard life experiences and see the lessons in them. Learn from those lessons to make healthier choices in the future.

A few months ago, I went back to school, and I received my Happiness Coaching Certificate. As a Happiness Coach, I want to help you learn to manage your own emotions, so you're able to find balance at any moment.

Wouldn't that feel good? Clarity, when you need it.

By allowing the traumas in my life to teach me hard lessons, and now armed with my training, it's time for me to guide others with what I've learned.

Just remember, you are enough, just as you are, in this very moment. You Are Enough.

My intentional healing journey began on my first day of therapy. I'll never forget it.

We had been on the road, living in our bus, for about two months. We were staying in Idyllwild, California at a Thousand Trails Campground. My emotions were all over the place. Kyle's depression was really taking its toll, the kids were young and demanded so much of my attention, and we kept having mechanical issues with the bus.

To say I was overwhelmed was a massive understatement.

On this mild early October early afternoon, I was at the pool texting with a friend from back home. She was telling me how her therapist was bringing down her overwhelm and helping her heal traumas in her past. At this point, I was at the end of my rope, so I asked for her therapist's number.

I texted her therapist, and I scheduled an introductory call for the following day. Honestly, I wasn't nervous about the call; I was exasperated and just wanted help. I'd take anything at this point.

"Jenn, you know the movie *Inside Out?* Do you remember Joy? You're Joy, Jenn. You don't want any other emotion in the driver's seat except for joy. You think that if you stay joyful, it'll all be okay, and you can get through it. That's a trauma response. Each emotion needs to be felt and validated." That was what my therapist said to me as we were wrapping up the end of our first therapy session call

I told the *Reader's Digest* version of my life, and she was right. I resonated so much with what she said that day. My kids watched that movie way too many times. On repeat in the back of our Honda Odyssey minivan. I'd never actually seen the movie— only heard it. That night I watched the movie from start to finish, and it clicked. To heal, I had to learn how to manage my emotions and let them each feel valid, then let them go.

This will be a piece of cake…I thought.

Beginning my healing journey was all about getting to know my emotions, why I was feeling a particular way in that moment, and from where it traced back.

Tracing it back to the cause was the most crucial step. I had to feel through the emotion, breathe, and follow the feeling back to a memory. Once I saw that memory, I was able to validate my emotion, forgive myself, give gratitude for the lesson, and let go of the pain.

Let me give you an example:

When my kids were younger, we would go to the outdoor playground for hours. It was a great way for them to burn off energy and for me to get to sit for a few minutes while they entertained themselves.

While at the playground, my kids would try to go up the slide backwards. As soon as I'd see them do this, I started to boil. The agitation was rising, and I was about to explode. It made me so angry to see them do this. If it happened, I would go over, completely enraged, and berate them for going up the slide. Why in the world would something this innocent and playful get me that worked up?

Let's trace it back.

When I was a young child, my father instilled following the rules down into my core. It was a very authoritarian type of parenting style my dad exhibited most of the time. He was very much a "you will obey me" kind of dad. Thinking back now, those words make me shudder in my soul. I digress.

There was one particular time when I was very young, maybe two or three. I was playing on our backyard slide. I started to go up it, and my dad came unglued. Yelling. Berating. "You DO NOT GO UP A SLIDE BACKWARDS!" Even now, remembering that moment, my body recoils.

Tracing further, I realized my agitation with my kids wasn't mine to carry. That was given to me by my dad, and I needed to decide if it was something I wanted to continue holding.

I took some breaths and asked myself, "Do I really care strongly about my kids going the wrong way?" No. No, I don't. I did, however, set some boundaries for safety. They at least had to look before climbing up to make sure someone wasn't coming down. Of course, they forgot once or twice, and a person smashed into them. It quickly reminded them to look next time.

After my conversation with myself, I was able to recognize where that emotion came from. Validate that emotion. Give my inner child a proverbial hug. I decided if I wanted to keep carrying that trauma or let it go. I modified it and let go of what I needed to, and I realized my dad was doing the best he could with what he had given his childhood upbringing.

The more I traced back, the more I would heal. I quickly realized that how I interacted with the world was directly related to how much unhealed trauma I had. The more trauma I healed, the lighter I felt, and the more I was able to manage my emotions in each moment.

Discovering true happiness is one of the greatest things I've found. The emotion of being happy isn't a destination. It means you're balanced in all of your emotions on the journey. So often, people feel like buying a new car will make them happy. If they get a promotion, it'll make them happier. If they lose weight, they'll be the happiest.

The thing is, if they keep that mindset, they'll never experience truly being happy. Happiness doesn't come from things; it's found by discovering your inner self.

How did I discover my inner self? I did it through getting to know my PTSD and healing childhood trauma.

With PTSD comes panic attacks. If you've ever experienced one, you know the sheer agony they bring you. You are legitimately concerned about your life at that moment. It's pure terror when everything is closing in around you, and you're struggling to breathe.

THE DAY THAT TIME STOOD STILL

September 16, 2011 started out as any other day. Ethan and I were making our daily walk up to his bus stop. Typically, I'd be wearing a robe, but since today was Friday, I was dressed in my dog-grooming attire. On Fridays, Kyle had off work from his warehouse job that paid most of the bills. But we needed a little more to survive; to earn extra money, I worked on Fridays at a local grooming salon.

This Friday though, it was extra special because of Ethan's 7th birthday on Monday! He asked for a weekend at Disney, so we booked a two-night stay at the Ramada Hotel in Kissimmee. As soon as I got home from work, the four of us would be hitting the open road for the fifty-minute trek to Walt Disney World.

Before Ethan hopped onto the bus, he picked me up a little yellow flower, a lantana. As he placed it in my hands, he said, "I love you, Mommy." I waved while he was taking his seat, and the bus pulled away.

I got home that afternoon around three, and the minivan was ready to go. We were all ecstatic about heading away for a couple nights and celebrating Ethan's birthday.

Our first stop was the Circle K to grab some Big Gulps, and we headed onto I-4.

We wouldn't make it to Disney World that day.

At 4:15 p.m., we were struck by a construction vehicle going westbound as we were heading east. The vehicle blew a tire and crossed the wires in the median. The flatbed on the truck grabbed onto our vehicle, and as we spun, the bed of the truck sliced down the entire driver side of our Chrysler Town & Country minivan.

When the spinning stopped as the cars separated, I saw Kyle stirring, still conscious with a head injury. I heard our thirteen-month old son Ben's screams in the seat behind me, so I knew he was okay. I didn't hear Ethan. There was so much debris; all I could see were his legs from the knee down and his black and gray Reebok ZigTech shoes.

I immediately leapt out of the van and ran to the driver's side. Ethan had been killed instantly, and I was immersed in the aftermath. I saw my child in a way that I hope no other parent has to experience. The last vision I have of Ethan is one I will carry with me for the rest of my life.

Because of the car accident that took the life of our son Ethan, I've had PTSD for nearly thirteen years. That's given me a lot of time to experience intense emotions and immensely real visuals. When I was first diagnosed, my states of being alternated between panic and overwhelm. It was twenty-four seven with no moments of peace, and we decided that I needed help from a psychiatrist.

Growing up, I never really was sick or had to take much medication. Aside from the occasional Tylenol or rare antibiotic, I consider myself blessed that I was a physically healthy kid. So, taking medication was foreign to me.

The psychiatrist I saw was extremely kind and supportive. He heard my expression of not wanting to be on heavy medicine long term, and we came up with a treatment plan. I'd take Benadryl when I needed to come down a level, and for the big panic attacks that got out of my control, I'd take Lorazepam.

What I found was that my panic was extremely high all the time. It was constantly getting out of control. (At this point in time, I didn't know control was an illusion, so I kept holding on tightly.) At the following month's appointment, we decided it was best if I went on a lower dose of Lorazepam every day for a few months. As much as I didn't want to be on medication, I made the choice to take it.

My psychiatrist was right.

During those first months after losing Ethan, I needed to be on autopilot. I needed to not feel anything. I needed to be numb. I needed to take that medicine.

I made the right choice.

What I've learned through that experience and many like it is that at every moment of my life, I've made the right choice for me. I needed to be on that medication for about six months, and then I was able to go down to a low-dose anxiety medication.

Eventually, I was able to work my way off the daily medication and managed everything myself.

I knew that I didn't want to be on medication forever, so I used it as a tool to reach my goal.

I was doing really well. I truly was. I was exercising every day, keeping the house clean, and even making dinner! About a year after the accident, we found out I was pregnant. We hadn't even been trying, but we traced it back to me forgetting a couple birth control pills that month. Once we wrapped our heads around the idea, so soon after losing Ethan, we were elated.

At twelve weeks, I miscarried, and our elation quickly turned into devastation.

That was hard on me. It was my second miscarriage. I had one before we got pregnant with Ben, and this one coming right after losing Ethan, made it even more difficult. I swore off having any other children. I didn't think I could handle any more heartbreak. Ben, our surviving son, was two at the time, and he became my focus.

Three months later, my period was late. I hadn't missed any pills recently. I hadn't been on antibiotics. It was peculiar, but I didn't think anything of it. I've had stretches where my periods were irregular, so this didn't seem unusual. A few days later, I started spotting.

After a day or two, the light spotting stopped. That was weird. Typically, my periods are super heavy and last anywhere from five to eight days. I had known that I was pregnant, but I brushed it off as my miscarriage might have gotten my regularly irregular cycle off track. Right? Yeah? Right.

Yeah, right.

My hunch was correct. I took a pregnancy test a few days later…and it was positive. Ready or not, we were having a Molly.

It took me a few months to get used to the idea that I was pregnant. Quite honestly, I was terrified to be having another baby. At this point, I'd lost Ethan and had two miscarriages, and my spirits were bleak. Deep down though, I had this little speck of light, just knowing my pregnancy would be perfectly fine.

And it was.

Life was grand for a few years after the accident. Kyle was working day shifts now at his job, I was staying at home with Ben and Molly, and we had so much time together as our little family of four. Shortly after Molly was born, we moved into a massive Victorian dollhouse type home—a whopping 3,300 square feet.

When Molly was one, I made the choice to do a "Mommy Makeover," where I got breast implants, a tummy tuck, and liposuction. After having three kids, my body had been transformed, and truthfully, I wanted to feel good about myself again. I don't regret getting plastic surgery; at that time, I was making the right decision for me at that moment.

Honestly, we loved it! I say we because both Kyle and myself benefited from my newfound confidence. We'd been having more fun together than we had in years. I felt so at home in my own body, a kind of feeling that's immensely difficult to put into words.

Speaking of feeling good, one late spring evening, in our spare bedroom after Ben and Molly were in bed, Kyle and I were having some really good fun.

Here's a little backstory: at this point in our marriage, we used condoms to prevent any more babies. I had recently found out birth control was messing with my health (another story for another day) and decided to stop taking the pill. Every time we had sex, though, we used protection. We didn't want any more babies. At this point, I was confident in my body, and my marriage was doing pretty well considering. We were content, and we didn't want to rock that boat given our history.

On this evening in our spare room, we were getting hot and heavy, and then it started feeling really good. Almost too good. Kyle finishes, and we then discover why that session felt so good.

The condom broke.

We were both adamant that we didn't want any more kids, so at 3 a.m., Kyle headed out to get the morning after pill after the condom initially broke.

SPOILER ALERT!

It was a warm July day near Washington DC, where we were on a six-week summer road trip in our RV. We were currently staying at Cherry Hill RV Resort having a delightful vacation.

Ben was around three and Molly eighteen months old, and we were content. We had two healthy babies, our marriage was doing well, and we were making such beautiful memories.

This particular day, I wasn't feeling too good. I started getting nauseous when I ate Caesar salad, which was very weird because I love Caesar salad.

I had a gut feeling. *Oh, no. No, no. Please, no.*

After promptly going to the store to buy a pregnancy test, I was coming out of the bathroom as Kyle had a bag of garbage in his hands, on the way to take it out. Our eyes met. He swallowed and got up the courage to ask, "Does it say *yes?*" I nodded. As the bag of trash fell from his hands, the word "Shit" fell out of his mouth. He looked devastated. Truthfully, I shared the same sentiments.

I was feeling such big emotions that at the time; I had no idea where they came from or what they were. I felt an immense amount of sadness for the contentment we just found; I knew it was all about to change. All the joy and happiness we were in all came crashing down around us.

Had I known then what I know now, I would've handled it much better. At this point on my journey, I know what my emotions are and how to manage them. Back then, I had big feelings, and I had no idea exactly how to work through them. That's the thing with hindsight: It makes you feel so much shame for making the best decisions for you in every moment.

I want to stress that reflecting on past growing opportunities and life lessons is very important to staying on your highway to happy. We must dive deep into our past in order to recognize it for what it is. Then, once we see it, we accept it. Accept what was done and know that you'd choose better given the same situation. After we have acceptance, forgiveness settles in, and we can let go of that blame, shame, or critical emotions and thoughts.

We were deeply struggling as a new family of five. Shortly before Eli was born, Kyle's depression started seeping in, and I felt more and more isolated. I knew Kyle wasn't thrilled about the idea of "starting over" with another baby. After the shock subsided, I was hopeful and happy we were sent this little miracle baby.

I went into labor around 3 a.m. with Eli, three weeks early. I'm typically scheduled for a C-section, but my doctors weren't listening to my early labor signs I was bringing up. I'd been to the hospital three times with false labor, and with as much scar tissue as I had from three previous C-sections at the time, I could hemorrhage if I went into active labor. I had some cause for concern.

Around six the previous evening, my neighbor came by, walking their dog on a Flexi leash. You know the bulky retractable leashes that are 25 feet long and recoil when you press a button? The dog, who is as sweet as can be and I genuinely loved, excitedly ran up to me and wrapped the Flexi leash around my ankles, causing me to wobble and fall over.

Luckily, I fell on my side and not my belly first. At first, I thought I was okay and went inside to rest. About a half hour went by, and I hadn't felt Eli kick. As you can imagine having lost a child, I went into an instant panic.

Kyle, who wasn't sharing my same concern, asked if I could get a friend to take me to the hospital because we had already been three times, and he didn't want to sit through another false alarm.

What you have to understand is at the time, Kyle was severely depressed from the unrecognized trauma of our accident with Ethan. He never saw a psychiatrist or counselor; he really didn't even open up to me about it. He carried this guilt of being the driver and never spoke a word about it to anyone. He was hurting so badly inside and feeling alone, so he began to disengage from life. This was the point that our marriage began to really crack and crumble.

One of my friends happily jumped at the opportunity to take me and potentially get to snuggle a baby, so off to the hospital we went!

As it turned out, Eli was perfectly fine! Thank goodness! I was having minimal and spontaneous little blurbs of contractions, but nothing they were concerned with, so back home we went.

However, when I woke up with awful pains at midnight, the little blurbs were now gigantic.

I really didn't want to wake Kyle up because I knew he'd be immensely agitated. In the back of my mind, I was telling myself, "It's all good, Jenn. This isn't labor. Just gas pains… maybe heartburn…."

When my contractions were ten minutes apart, my brain couldn't keep denying the fact I was in labor. When I first woke Kyle up at 4 a.m., he didn't believe that this was, in fact, not a false alarm. He told me he would take me, but he had to take a shower first, so I would have to wait.

While Kyle was showering, I called his mom, and she came rushing in the door to stay with our older two kids. When she walked in, she saw me on the couch, mid contraction and in intense pain. She looked at me, instantly knew I was in active labor, and asked where Kyle was. I told her that he'd been in the shower for about forty-five minutes, and I was waiting for him to get out. She turned on her heels and marched into our master bathroom. I'd never heard my mother-in-law ever be that loud before. "Kyle! Jennifer is in labor! Get out here and get her to the hospital!" I'll admit, it felt good to hear that and have a mom in my corner.

We were finally on our way to the hospital around 5:30 a.m. The last time I had contractions was with Ethan back in 2004. To say I didn't miss them was an understatement. Once we got up to the labor and delivery floor, I was whisked away to prep for an emergency C-section, and Kyle went to get prepped in his gear.

It was a whirlwind. People were running around; I was being asked a ton of questions, and I couldn't see Kyle. They kept numbing me, but I could still feel their painful poking. My anxiety started to climb. I think at one point it was reaching maximum panic, and I remember falling asleep.

When I came to, Kyle was standing by an incubator with what felt like ten people, with a baby, not making a noise. Cue more panic.

The anesthesiologist noticed that I was confused and my anxiety was rising. As they were trying to reassure me, Eli let out a wail, and I exhaled.

I really believe this is where my resentment began for the way Kyle, in deep depression, began to treat me. The evening Eli was born, at around twelve hours after the surgery, I needed to go to the bathroom. About ten minutes before, Kyle said he needed to get out of this hospital room, and he was going out. My sister would be coming up within the hour, and I didn't really want to be left alone. He insisted he needed to go, so off he went. It was just me and Eli, sleeping in his bassinet.

The issue at hand was I had to go pee. Really. Really. Really. Bad. They'd already taken my catheter out; I was going to have get to the toilet. I called the nurse. No answer. Crap. I waited. I really had to go. I called back. The nurse said she was busy at the moment, and I'd have to go myself.

Not knowing when anyone would be in the room to help me, I began the painful process of getting up and out of bed.

I think that was the most physically painful thing I've ever had to find the strength to do. I do not recommend getting up and trying to walk by yourself to the bathroom within twelve hours of having major surgery that cuts your entire stomach open. It felt as if burning hot knives were slicing into my abdomen while my freshly cut open skin was screaming in agony with every little hunched over step I took. Hindsight, I should've just peed in bed.

I painstakingly made it to the toilet just in time to feel the exhilarating rush of emptying my bladder into it. Of course, Eli began screaming at the top of his lungs as the final drip landed in the bowl. I sat there for a moment, contemplating all my life choices ever. I took a breath in, and I was ready to do this.

Just as I was about to hoist myself up my sister walked in. As you can imagine, she was furious. Luckily, she wasn't mad at me because it's illegal to be angry with women who have just given birth, and she graciously helped me back to bed and made me remain there for the duration of the evening.

Kyle came back a couple of hours later, looking pretty refreshed. He had rented a bike and rode around town, not knowing the exponential pain I had just experienced.

For many years, I held resentment with him for that moment in time. Because of his childhood trauma, combined with the trauma of losing Ethan, he didn't have the capacity for care when Eli was born. Kyle was barely keeping his head above water, trying to do his best. Of course, with hindsight, therapy, and an enormous amount of self-reflection, I'm able to see that now. The Jenn back then was also doing her best too. I've learned to forgive every version of myself, every season, every day, every minute, every second; I know I am and have always been doing the best I could.

You have too.

Of course, the Jenn of today is a more evolved version than the season I was in at the time of Eli's birth. The beautiful thing is sitting in the present moment and reflecting on climbing all those peaks and valleys you've grown through to get where you are today. Sometimes, I like to sit in that for a little while, soaking in the warmth of being proud of myself. I think a lot of times in society, we are taught to push down the things we are proud of about ourselves because it makes us look less humble. Knowing that all the things can be happening all at once, and all of them are okay, is the beauty of duality.

The days went by, and time marched on.

I truly believe this is where our marriage completely shattered.

The kids were growing and entering into extracurricular activities, which meant less and less time we spent together as a family and as a couple.

When Kyle was growing up, he played Little League and travel baseball. As a baby, our son Ben gravitated to the sport just like Kyle did. Once Kyle saw Ben had an interest, they practiced and played together every day. Kyle began to coach Ben's Little League teams followed by travel baseball. As you can imagine, this took up so much of our lives. In addition to Ben doing baseball three to five days a week, Molly was in art once a week, and they both had a reading tutor twice during the week. The weekends were always filled with the family attending Ben's baseball games. He usually had a tournament three weekends out of the month, so it didn't leave much time for anything else. We continued this way for about four years after we had Eli until we reached a breaking point.

Looking back, 2019 was a year of disruption and chaos. It was our year that all the unhealed trauma caused us to have BIG emotions and spew our anger, resentment, and hatred all over each other. Kyle and I were suffering in so many ways, and we had no idea what was happening internally and subconsciously. We were taking out on each other everything that we hadn't healed. Everything that we hadn't healed we were taking out on the other person.

I truly believe we always hurt the ones we love the most because we give all of ourselves to them. Our happy side, sad side, angry side, resentful side, joyful side, fearful side—all the sides. Yes, even the messy side of us too. Our partners see more sides of us than anyone else will. They are with us more than anyone, sharing each other's energies. We become bonded to that person, and they'll always be a part of our highway even if you aren't together anymore. Their memory always remains.

Their memory is their energy with you. Everyone you meet or interact with leaves you with their energy. It could feel good or not vibe with you; it can even be kind of ambivalent. There's an old saying, you don't always remember the words a person says to you, but you always remember how they made you feel. How you make someone feel is from your energy.

We all have an aura, also considered an energetic field, around us. Every living thing does. Think about it for a second: When you meet a new person, your gut instantly tells you if this person has a positive, negative, or indifferent energy. The more I have gotten out in nature and sat in silence, the more I've been able to tune into that gut-feeling energy. The more I've asked myself hard questions that I feared the answer to, the more I got to know myself and who I am.

The year 2019 was also the catalyst for me begging to acknowledge my healing journey that led me onto my highway to happy. Aside from 2011, when we lost Ethan, 2019 was the most difficult year to date. When we were in it, going through that experience, I had no idea how much it cracked me open to bloom into who I am now.

I reframed each individual struggle that I've had from a negative mindset of shame, guilt, resentment to one of pride, forgiveness, and empowerment. Through my life in the pages of this book and what I've grown through, by the end of it, you'll learn how you can reframe your mindset too.

Picture it: May of 2018, it is late spring in Florida, and the wildflowers are wilting as the temperatures are heating up. Eli is three, Molly is five, and Ben will be eight in August. Kyle and I are celebrating our tenth wedding anniversary at the end of the month with a big vow renewal.

Since we initially got married in Las Vegas, my request at the time was to get a huge vow renewal for our tenth anniversary. I'd hired an event planner to make the entire process

less stressful on me because I was running my own pet salon
at the time.

To this day, Jenn's Pup 'n Suds (JPS), my pet salon, remains one of
my most proud accomplishments. For years, I'd dreamt of opening
my own dog grooming salon. I started working for PetSmart in 2005
and worked my way up from dog bather to groomer, then salon manager, and eventually an academy instructor, where I hosted academies,
teaching students to become groomers. Being a grooming instructor
was where I found so much joy. I am a huge animal advocate, so being able
to share a passion of mine focusing on safety really sparked my fire.

Being a single Mom with Ethan, I had to work. When we had Ben back
in 2010, I knew I wanted to stay at home with him. I put my two weeks'
notice in and never went back to PetSmart. I did, however, work in private
salons through the years on Kyle's days off for extra money at the time.
We always wanted someone to be at home with the kids, and I have an
immense amount of gratitude for Kyle and myself working together to
be able to make that happen.

In late 2017 I opened up JPS in our backyard. I had a cute little finished shed that I started out of. Kyle and his grandpa helped build,
insulate, wire, and make it come to life. My little salon was painted
a muted shade of blue with darker gray trim and a white door. It had an
A-frame roof with an adorable umbrella patio set out front. Finishing
its exterior cuteness, I decorated it with cheerful plants and a cute
little sign.

By the time of our vow renewal in mid-2018, I had amassed a
large clientele and had already needed to expand the salon. Business was
booming as my marriage was crumbling.

In the days, weeks, and months coming up, they'd be some
of the darkest of my life. I turned to alcohol to numb my PTSD,

the night terrors, and the abandonment I felt from Kyle. At the time, my work ethic was ingrained into me. I had to work to provide for my family. Some days I'd be in the salon at 6:30 a.m. and not walk back in the door to the house until well after 8 p.m. It was fantastic to have a full clientele, though not as great to be on your feet for ten to twelve hours a day. Needless to say, my energy levels were non-existent when I got home. Nevertheless, I was grateful I had a short commute to work.

Once I came in for the day, Kyle had already left with Ben for baseball practice, which meant Eli and Molly were with me.

Kyle was so deep into depression at this point, the only thing I can compare him to is a mostly emotionless zombie just existing in the world. Farming didn't work out with his dad, so he became Mr. Mom. I went to work, and he took the kids to school and shuttled them to their activities. During the day, he would come home, occasionally help me if I needed it in the salon, or he would play video games and sleep.

Kyle was so despondent and removed from our marriage. I continued to try to change and bend to fit what he needed, so he could be happy again. What I didn't see back then was that neither one of us were responsible for the other one's happiness. I recall being so resentful to him for never making an effort to give me what I needed to feel loved. The more I gave him what he needed, the less he gave me.

With our packed schedule, quality time together or as a family was non-existent. It began to really take its toll on me, and I never wanted to be home. I spent as much time as I could pouring into my dog grooming business. At the time, it felt like everything was such a mess, and the summer of 2019 was the beginning of the end.

THE END OF US

For the previous few summers, we would take an extended trip in our RV as a family. We started doing that shortly after Ethan passed away. For many reasons that we didn't realize at the time, being on the road and camping were some of our absolute best times. We all got along, we worked together, and we turned so many moments into memories.

The summer of 2019, we'd been planning a month-long trip up to Tennessee to see my sister and then back down to Florida. Honestly, we had another phenomenal trip together. We dreaded going back to our "regular lives" and dreamed of staying on the road, leaving everything behind.

We pulled into the driveway of our then "dream home" that we'd spent over a year completely renovating. At the time, we thought this was the pinnacle; this is what we've been working for our entire lives. This big, beautiful house, successful entrepreneurs, brand new cars, a large beach-entry pool with a sprawling two acres of land in one of the most populated counties in Florida.

By society's standards, we'd "made it."

As I was schlepping a suitcase from the RV bedroom to Kyle by the door, he turned and looked at me, his face calm but serious. It caught me off guard. Little did we know the question he asked me next would change the entire course of our lives.

"What if we sold everything we owned, bought a vintage bus, then remodeled it, and we can travel full time with the kids?"

That was not what I expected to come out of his mouth. I remember letting out this weird snort-laugh-whimper noise before I replied, "That would be amazing. But we can't. We have a life here. I have a salon here. You aren't supposed to do that until you retire. No. We can't."

And off Kyle went, his hopes and dreams slayed by yours truly.

From the moment he turned away, something cracked inside me and a seed was planted. This little seed of hope. A hope that our family could be saved. A hope that our marriage could be repaired. A hope that we could truly experience contentment and inner peace in our life.

The day after we got home, I returned to work at my salon. I'm sure you know, when you leave for a long trip and come back, it's utter chaos. Even though I was remotely running it, there were still so many tasks left undone. Needless to say, I was over it.

Amid the overwhelm, I kept dreaming about being at the Grand Canyon with the kids. I kept thinking about going to Yellowstone and seeing Old Faithful erupting. I began to resent all of the time doing this nine-to-five daily grind and what it took from my life. In that moment, I realized, this "perfect life," just-to-be-frank, sucked. I was wasting my life and time with my kids and my partner living for other people's perspectives.

Two weeks from the day that Kyle asked me that fateful question, I came in from the salon, and I walked directly up to him. I looked him in the eye, and I said, "Let's do it. Let's buy a bus, sell everything we own, travel the country, and save our family." I knew deep in my soul this was the direction we needed to turn our family in.

You must understand at the time, the relationship I had with Kyle then, we were both doing the best we could with what we had, still surrounded by societal "goals."

We were making decisions for our lives based on the things that were expected of us by our parents, our friends, our neighbors; basically, making decisions for everyone but ourselves.

We didn't think therapy was an option since we grew up being told you're "crazy," and "there's something wrong with you" if you go to any kind of therapy. We didn't really have the capacity to hear each other out let alone make a clear decision to recognize we needed therapy.

There are so many *coulda-shoulda-wouldas* that we can all look back on our lives that tell us what we might choose differently next time. Me choosing to push for bus-life and living an alternative lifestyle to save my family will always be a decision I'm so proud that I made.

Starting out was a bumpy road.

So, we had this idea that bus life was going to save us. The problem that I've learned with looking for something to save you is that you don't do the work to help save yourself. You're waiting for something else to do it, and if that's the case, your saving is never going to come.

At least, that was my experience.

From August to November of 2019, we had been deeply purging all of the things in chaos as usual. You see, we have never really been planners, but were more of doers. Both Kyle and I learn best by jumping in and getting our hands dirty.

Did we formulate a genius and well-thought-out plan for bus life from start to finish, mapping out every minute detail?

Absolutely not.

Kyle and I sat down and did what we always do. We picked out the major things that had to be done, and we did little things each day to accomplish them. We didn't plan out what the little things were; we just subconsciously did them one by one. Until one day, all our belongings were sold, and our house was on the market. We'd remodeled and moved into our bus, and then COVID came.

There was someone way back in ancient times, in a different land, who knew that a flood was coming, and he needed to build a boat to save their family.

As they were building this boat, people would laugh at what they were doing. Word had spread through their small village that they were building a boat to save their family from the flood. They'd advise the villagers to save themselves and build their own boat to save their own families. Again, the villagers just laughed.

As they expected, because they'd already moved into their boat because of their inner knowing, the flood came, and they saved their family. Bringing them to a new life together.

Our bus was our boat.

I didn't realize it back then, but what we naturally did actually worked. I listened and followed my inner knowing, and it got us to the life of our dreams. We didn't have a detailed plan; we identified big things and took little bites out of them every day.

At the end of August 2019, we made the decision to do bus life. The day before Eli's birthday in February 2020, we moved into our fully remodeled home on wheels, Blue Betty. In just six short months, we literally kissed everything we knew goodbye and set out down the road, merging onto our highway to happy.

In recent years, I've come to realize for myself that time is a human made construct that didn't exist until we made it up. If time is going to pass either way, I choose to spend mine making it count.

THE BOULEVARD OF BROKEN DREAMS

In March of 2020 the world as we knew it felt like it stopped spinning. When the Facebook memes go from mockery to mourning, the outlook is bleak.

In April of 2020, we put our "dream house" on the market after sprucing it up. Because we had just moved into our bus and so much uncertainty hung in the air, we thought it was best to move our bus to Kyle's parents' property roughly fifteen minutes away. This way, our sprawling ranch home could be listed and shown without a big bus in the driveway.

Moving to the farm had its challenges; we knew it wasn't going to be easy, but it was needed. We truly wanted to hit the road and begin our adventure; it just didn't feel like the right time to do it.

So, we waited.

Looking back, it was a beautiful time of patience. Having this extra breathing room gave our house time to sell and for us to add the solar panels onto our bus. You know when businesses do a "preview" or "trial period" before doing their grand opening?

I see this time as our "soft launch" season, lol.

Spending four months on Kyle's parents' farm gave us an opportunity to try on Bus Life and see if we really were able to coexist in that small of a space as a family of two adults, three kids, and four dogs.

I think with COVID looming over everything, this time period was different for us. Honestly, it felt like we were in this protected bubble, and we were just grateful to be together because others were losing so much around us. Their businesses, homes, and most importantly their loved ones.

We'd just sold our house, so we were in decent financial shape. Everyone's daily routine was disrupted, so sitting and being became the new normal. We spent time playing board games and connecting with each other.

Not only were we there, but Kyle's brother, parents, and grandpa were too. Every night, Kyle or his parents would cook dinner, and we'd all meet over at their house. We would sit around the table and talk about memories made and times gone by.

By August of 2020 though, we were ready to hit the road and spread our wings, the taste of freedom ever so close. We felt like it was safe to go out into the world if we were cautious. We took a couple weeks to pack everything up, pare things down, and prepare to live our lives on the road.

FAILURE TO LAUNCH DAY

August 6, 2020 was an exciting day to say the least. Today was THE day that we'd be hitting the road in our new home on wheels, and the excitement was palpable!

Let me set the scene for you....

The electricity of chaos was in the air. We were running around Kyle's parents' farm, trying to remember all the little things we needed to make sure were in the bus. At the last minute, Kyle wanted to wash the bus because it was her maiden voyage, so she needed to look fresh. As he was using the hose to douse Blue Betty down, I am wrangling dogs and kids, herding them onto our new mobile house on wheels.

Finally, we're all on board and the engine was humming; we wave our goodbyes to our family and off we went!

It had been the plan all along to make a stop at our mechanic's shop for some routine maintenance, an oil change, tires rotated—a little once over. His shop was only two hours north of Kyle's parent's place.

Kyle had been driving the bus with the kids while I was following behind in our jeep. One of the routine maintenance things we'd been stopping here for was installing our towing lights, so we all could be in the bus traveling together.

Shortly after pulling into our mechanics shop, our amazingly great moods went south quickly....

Our mechanic's head was discouragingly shaking from side to side as he delivered the bad news. Our bus has torsion bars that are for the suspension, and these bars hadn't been made for these buses since at least 1997. He was honestly surprised we made it the two-hour drive without our left rear bar snapping. He said that he could fix it and get us back on the road, but he would need at least a couple of weeks to source a torsion bar to fit.

This would be an incredibly labor-intensive job, and the part wouldn't come cheap either. He estimated we'd be looking at around $6,500 and three weeks to get it finished.

Well, shit.

We really didn't have another choice, so we left Blue Betty there and packed up our four dogs, three kids, and enough belongings for a couple weeks in our Jeep Grand Cherokee and made the two-hour drive back south to stay in Kyle's childhood bedroom.

This lesson was honestly crucial in our journey. I remember sitting on their backyard swing, my bare feet in the dirt, with the mechanic's words swirling in my head. "I'm surprised you made it two hours on this thing."

In that moment, I felt an immense amount of gratitude that we made it. I genuinely believe my mechanic's tone of concern when he was going over what he found with us. That situation could have been so much worse, but it wasn't. As I was soaking in that gratitude, I promised myself that I'd find thankfulness in the smallest of things from now on.

✋ HIGHWAY TO HAPPY: REST STOP #1

✦ Give Gratitude ✦

That moment was really the first step to living on my highway to happy every single day. I was able to remove myself from the big emotions of fear, worry, and regret to focus on my gratefulness that we were okay. I knew in my heart in that moment, I needed to continue to find gratitude in the smallest of ways, and it would help me greatly on my healing journey.

This is what I did:

I got grounded. Whenever the big emotions of fear, worry, guilt, shame, blame, criticism, and so many other heavy ones bubble up, I take my shoes off and put my feet in the grass. I feel the cool dirt upon my feet, and I shift my awareness to my breathing. Just feeling my lungs go up and then fall back down with my exhale.

I bring my awareness to my feet, and I feel the earth's energy slightly buzz as I ask myself to name something for which I am grateful.

"I am grateful for the clean oxygen in my lungs," I say to myself.

I think of something else I am grateful for.

"I am grateful I have food in my pantry today," I feel myself saying.

By the third or fourth item for which I feel gratitude, I am experiencing fewer and less heavy emotions and more joyful ones. Being out of the bigger and heavy emotions, I can have clarity and recognize just how blessed I really am. That scary or big thing doesn't have a hold on me anymore if I give gratitude to it.

What are three things you can give gratitude to, right now in this very moment?

Take all the time you need.

GROWING DOWN THE ROAD

Luckily, our second launch day went much more smoothly than the last, and we were about two months into living on the road at this point. What we quickly realized is that our problems didn't exactly go away. With our Hail Mary of Bus Life, they were magnified. When you go from 2,000 square feet to living in 320, little things become big problems relatively quickly.

Kyle and I were doing better than we were in a house; that is for sure. However, we were far from doing well as a couple and as individuals. I made the decision to begin seeing an individual therapist because Kyle declined to go to a couple's therapist. I knew that I needed help, and I couldn't worry about whether he was going to go or not.

THE CATALYST TO HEALING MY SOUL

Remember my first therapy session I spoke of at the beginning of my highway?

"Jenn, you've seen the movie *Inside Out* haven't you? Do you remember the character Joy? You are Joy, Jenn." My therapist said to me at the end of our very first call.

She wasn't saying it as a complement, and I knew it. In that instant, I realized this was going to be an entirely individual journey for me. In the movie, Joy wanted everything to all be okay all the time. Joy worked tirelessly to make sure that no other emotion was able to be felt or seen. If Joy was okay, everyone else was okay. Ultimately, Joy had to investigate her own shadow and allow other emotions to be felt and worked through in order to live an emotionally healthy life.

I never watched that movie the same way again.

Truth be told, that was one of the most powerful things anyone has ever said to me, and I needed to hear it. Before beginning therapy, I felt like I was handling all the things and taking on all the burdens—because I was. I was taking on things and emotions that weren't mine and neglecting to bring light to the ones that were.

I spent most of my time always wanting to live in joy. I never really gave any of my other emotions time to be valid, feel seen, and most importantly heard. Without hearing my emotions out, I was stuffing that subconscious trauma attached to them under a rug, along with my hurt emotions.

I was perpetuating this cycle of being burnt out from feeling this need of trying to make everyone happy but me. Then, everyone else was feeling good because they were taken care of, but that led them to being unaware that I needed to be taken care of.

When my therapist told me that, it shifted my focus to me and my emotions that need to be managed first before I can collaborate with other people. I was responsible for my own actions. I was responsible for my own choices. I was responsible for bringing my balanced self to all my relationships.

The old adage really is true: You have to put your oxygen mask on first. Going to individual therapy was the beginning of resuscitating my family by starting with me individually.

I never would've thought…

If you would've told me five years ago that by me simply going to therapy for my individual self and putting into practice what I've learned into my everyday life would begin to change my family members around me, I would have never believed it was possible.

Sure, in theory it sounds very simple, but it's anything but easy. My thought was that time is going to pass either way, and I'd rather spend those minutes making it count.

I'd been going to individual therapy for about six weeks when one day Kyle asked if he could speak to me outside.

The previous day, we had our biggest falling out as a couple yet. Throughout mine and Kyle's marriage, he has stopped taking certain medications without telling me. This was the fourth time he had done so, and it had been two months since he had taken his medication.

I could already tell something was amiss with him for several weeks now, but every time I approached him, he used gaslighting to get the subject dropped. I was early on in my therapy journey, and I was doing my best to navigate life in a rolling home while being a mom and a partner. This was the most I'd ever juggled at once in my life; now Kyle had stopped taking the essential medication that he needed, and he was feeling physically and mentally lousy. He felt so bad that he asked me to drive him to the emergency room because he felt like he was dying.

As it turned out, the terrible nausea, panic, and whole-body aches were coming from withdrawals from not having his medicine that he stopped without telling anyone.

Kyle was now standing in front of me at an RV Park in Acton, California, his eyes filled with sadness.

"I know I need to turn my life around," he somberly said. "You don't deserve the man I am now. You and the kids deserve me at my best, and that's what I want to be. Do you think we could go to couple's therapy?"

He was trying. He truly was making an effort by having the courage to come to me, get vulnerable, and ask that question. My heart knew the answer, and the next day I texted my therapist asking if she would see us as a couple.

She happily answered, "Absolutely."

THE LITTLE WHITE VAN

The days turned into weeks and the weeks into months; before we knew it, we'd been on the road, still living in our bus and traveling the country as a family for a year and a half.

Since the beginning of our journey, we had been vlogging it on YouTube and posting our life's experiences on social media. We genuinely wanted to show that a life on your own terms was possible through living by example and showing what we did.

We've always been really open about our mental health online, and therapy was one of those things we frequently talked about. I'd write posts about finding time to go to therapy, and we would include it in our vlogs. Therapy had been a miracle for Kyle and me. As a couple, were growing together more and more every day. We still had a long way to go, but the important thing was that we were doing it as a team. As long as we both were trying, we could grow through anything....

On August 27, 2021 we were leaving at Fulltime Families Rally in Yellowstone National Park, and we were asking our friends where to go. Our friends Shelly and Ryan told us that we had to go to the Tetons and camp in the Spread Creek camping area. Since we fly by the seat of our pants and are pretty flexible, we took their advice. It would be a cool adventure!

As we set out that day, our Jeep was being towed behind our bus, and we were all riding together when Kyle noticed a problem with the shifting and pulled the bus over. He found a large piece of dry cardboard in the ditch to lay on and went under the bus.

When he emerged, he said a linkage needed to be replaced, but he had no replacement part, and we were out in the middle of nowhere with no cell signal. In that moment, I remembered seeing a funny little piece in Kyle's toolbox while I was looking for a wrench he needed a few minutes ago.

I ran to his toolbox, grabbed this little thingy that looked like a fancy "0" then rushed back to Kyle by the back tires. "Is this what you need?" He had a huge grin spread across his face as he said, "Yup!"

We were back on the road after a couple hours delay. This wouldn't ordinarily be a big deal; however, we needed to get there by no later than sundown. Trying to park in the dark in the wilderness with no cell signal is one of our cardinal "no nos."

I still remember this feeling of knowing we needed to be there; I just didn't know why.

As we drove through Jackson Hole, I was skeptical we were going to make it before dark. I kept pleading with the universe to please get us there, please get us there....

Just then, the Grand Tetons came into view.

Majestic. Purely majestic. When they sang "purple mountain majesty," they were talking about these beauties. I was flabbergasted by their massive size and eccentric sawtooth shape. "There's the freakin' Tetons!" I shouted in the video. I can still feel my excitement at this moment.

If you've never seen or heard of them, put this book down right now and Google them. Are they not just breathtaking?

After experiencing them, a sense of calm washed over me. It was all going to be okay. We would get there in time; I remember that comfortable feeling. The rest of the ride was so beautiful; we all sat together as Kyle drove our home down the highway, and we soaked up that happy moment.

After our first attempt at a spot failed miserably, we had unhitched the Jeep, and I was driving behind the bus. I saw Kyle put on his right turn signal at an old wooden sign with the letters "SPREAD CREEK" carved into it.

It was about 6:00–6:15 p.m., and the sun was slowing sinking into the horizon. As I'm driving, the bus is kicking up clouds of dirt, making it difficult to see far. I just kept following Kyle's tail lights.

When Kyle was driving the bus, he liked to capture footage with our GoPros. He would have one facing forward and one to him. He'd talk to the viewers while pointing out things he found interesting. On this particular day, as we pulled into the spread creek, he forgot to turn them off when he was finished recording.

I followed the bus about two miles down this bumpy, rocky desert road, and now we were reaching clumps of taller trees, making a canopy over the road. I can remember thinking, "It sure was beautiful in here," as we came up to a little white van parked in a camping spot along the creek. What stood out to me was that it had Florida plates. I made a mental note to tell Kyle that when we got parked, I'd like to go meet whoever had driven that van.

We drove deeper and deeper down this bumpy road to no avail. There wasn't a spot for us to park anywhere. As Kyle was turning the bus around, I called him.

"Hey, did you see that van with Florida plates?!" We both shouted at the same time to each other. After we giggled about that, he said, "Let's park in the big gravel lot up front. On the way up, want to stop and say hi if they are back? It looked pretty closed when we went by."

As we pulled past the little white van, in the same little camping spot, it still looked closed up. Kyle decided to keep driving, and I followed him a couple of miles up to the big gravel lot. We cooked dinner because everyone was starving; then we all trudged off to bed, exhausted from our day. We planned to leave the next morning about 9 a.m., as we were making our way to South Dakota for my upcoming tattoo appointment. I'd had my tattoo appointment scheduled for the better part of a year. I found an amazing tattoo artist on a whim to give me a half sleeve of flowers. They represented each of our little family's birth flowers. I wanted to add to my arm and knew I had to wait for her to do it.

As it so happened, we had planned to work the Beet Harvest in North Dakota beginning in late September with our friends Jed and Sandy. As we are driving on the highway leaving Rapid City, South Dakota and heading to Bismarck, North Dakota, information begins to trickle out on social media about a missing VanLife girl and her boyfriend.

FBI, HOW CAN I DIRECT YOUR CALL?

A few weeks have gone by, and there's a lot of news about a missing VanLife girl, Gabby Petito. She was said to have gone missing in the Tetons earlier in August. I had remembered news reports saying she was there August 17 or 18.

I was watching a news video of a man in his forties speaking about his missing daughter, Gabby. I looked to the left on the screen and saw Gabby's mom, and I felt this instant connection to her. It felt like I knew her; my mind explained it away as one mom connecting with another over a mom's biggest fear. I sent some loving energy her way and clicked off the video.

The month of September is a difficult one for us because of the anniversary of our son's death and, three days later, his birthday. To get through the tough month, I started a campaign called Pay it Forward for Ethan. It's when we encourage everyone to do a random act of kindness for someone each day during the month of September. This particular year, we planned to partner with Mental Health America and raise money for their non-profit. We'd also be donating all our AdSense, the money we make from YouTube, for the month as well.

Basically, the more views we get, the more money we can donate. At the time, our views were making us about $200 a month, and we were happy to help and do our part too.

It was September 18, and we were camping that night in a Walmart parking lot in Bismarck, North Dakota. I was editing our next day's YouTube video. It happened to be the footage of our one evening in the Grand Tetons at Spread Creek. We were en route the next day to meet our dear friends Jed and Sandy to work the Great Sugar Beet Harvest.

I was just about to close my laptop at 11:58 p.m. when my iPhone buzzed on the desktop. I had this nudge to check what the notification was, so I did.

The alert was from my friend Sarah. She had tagged me in an Instagram story from the National Park Service stating the timeline had changed in the search for Gabby Petito. They had asked if anyone had footage from Spread Creek on August 27 or 28 to please look through it.

Oh, shit. My stomach sank.

I flipped open my laptop open, and it was 12:01 a.m. on September 19. Ethan would be turning seventeen. This thought came across my mind as I was scanning through my memory card. I knew it was here; I just knew it.

Earlier, when I was editing, I had noticed that Kyle had forgotten to turn the GoPros off. I skimmed through the footage, and it didn't yield any talking, so I didn't add it to the video. Now though, I remembered seeing something....

I yelled for Kyle. "Babe! Get up now! Please!" He jolted out of bed, and as he stood next to me, I calmly said, "I think we have her van."

We watched the footage of the GoPro together, and a little white speck came into view. I remember thinking, "Please make it, please make it." You see, GoPro doesn't have a great battery life, and these cameras should have stopped recording minutes ago. Yet somehow, they were still rolling, the little white speck getting clearer and clearer.

As we saw our bus cameras clearly capture the van in its entirety, forward and rear facing, I let out a gasp.

"That's her van. That's her van, Jenn. Oh, my god. That's her van," Kyle said wearily as he put his hands to his head to steady himself.

I was already dialing the FBI tip line as Kyle was wobbling. "Hello, FBI, how can I direct your call?"

"Yes! Yes! I have her van! I have footage of Gabby Petito's van! Patch me over to a detective please!" I hurriedly exclaimed.

"You drop any footage you have to the link on the website, and someone will contact you," she said.

"I don't think you understand—I have her van! I have footage of her van on video! The missing girl, Gabby Petito. I have her van!" I protested.

"Yes ma'am, all the tips are going there. Please put them in the link." Hearing the annoyance in her voice, as calmly as I could through gritted teeth, I said, "thank you."

When I hung up, I turned to Kyle and asked, "What do we do now?" He looked at me with eyes so sure of himself and asked, "What does your gut tell you to do?"

I didn't know what anyone else would do. As a mom who has lost a child, I knew what I would want someone to do for me if there was a chance of the child coming home alive.

"We need to get this footage out as fast and as far as possible to help find her."

I threw together a two-minute video with the footage and us voicing over our experience with the details we had. We had a vlog I was just about to upload, so I decided to throw this little video before any of our video. That way, people could watch what they needed from our clip, then go about their day.

By 9 a.m. the next day, the video had more than a million views. It was blowing up and so were our phones. News outlets in not only our country but all over the world were texting, calling, emailing, and trying to find any way possible to get ahold of us for an interview.

"What have I done?" I thought. We were in the middle of an epic whirlwind of emotions when Kyle walked into my room.

"Nichole emailed you, Jenn. Gabby's Mom. She wants to talk to you...."

Oh, crap. Did I do the wrong thing? Is she going to yell at me? Oh, please don't be angry, I just did what I would have wanted done to me…these were all things my anxiety was attached to, and my thoughts were running wild.

I took a deep breath in, stood up, and I walked out to our kitchen to read it. She wanted me to call her, and so I did.

Instantly, as the FaceTime screen picked up, I knew why I connected to her on the TV interview video.

Thankfully, she wasn't mad at all, and I was grateful. I asked her one question: "What do you need? I will do anything."

She needed to find her daughter, and she asked me to do as many national interviews as I could to try and help find her. And so that is what I did.

I vividly remember riding on my bed in the bus, while it was gray and rainy outside, doing a Fox News interview going down the road. We were on our way to Fargo, North Dakota meeting up with Jed and Sandy, heading off to Grafton together the following morning.

As we pulled into the Costco parking lot, I couldn't wait until Sandy pulled in to get one of her world-famous hugs. Her hug did not disappoint, and it felt so good to have another human's touch. What Sandy and Jed did for us in the weeks after what happened I will forever be grateful and hold those memories close to my soul.

Looking back on that day we found the footage was all so surreal. It was like having a dream, and you wake up wondering, "Did that really happen?"

Yes, it did, and it was about to get deeper.

That night we ended up parking at a Walmart down the street from the Costco where we met up with Sandy and Jed. It was Ethan's birthday, so we invited them to join us outside in our lawn chairs, sing "Happy Birthday" to Ethan, and then eat cake. They happily obliged, and as we were finishing up our delectable chocolate cake with buttercream frosting, my phone rang....

I had been receiving calls nonstop from news outlets. They'd found Gabby's remains shortly after I met Sandy and Jed for a much-needed hug. They were right where they needed to be at exactly the right time. After being alerted to the footage we captured back on August 27; they were able to find Gabby just a few hours after sunlight once they saw our video.

Here I was in a Walmart parking lot with my phone ringing, and I knew this call was different, and I needed to answer.

"Hello?" I said shakily.

"Jenn? Jenn, this is Joe. Joe Petito, Gabby's dad," the caller said.

The conversation I had with Joe is another that will live in my soul forever. We both had so much gratitude as we got to speak with each other. I knew from that day that Gabby must have been a very special, one-of-a-kind soul with beautiful parents like these.

I was grateful for anything we could do to help.

SERENDIPITOUS DAY

Nearing the end of September, we were in Grafton, North Dakota with our friends Jed and Sandy as well as Jessa, Dan, and their son B. Being able to spend these last couple weeks after finding the footage with our amazing friends truly helped us stay balanced and sane. Without them, I don't think we would have been able to make it through as well as we did.

Jessa and Dan lived fulltime in their vintage travel trailer.

Jed and Sandy in their Campervan, then us in our bus, Blue Betty. We were here because of the Great Sugar Beet Harvest, a work-camping opportunity to spend a few weeks assisting in the sugar beet harvesting process.

The association you work for typically provides you with an RV site for the duration of your employment at no cost to you. Jed, Sandy, and Kyle were working the harvest while Jessa, Dan, and I were hanging out. We had campfires every night and shared meals with each other. The short time before the harvest started was pure bliss. It was exactly what we needed after what had transpired the previous two weeks.

The news hadn't gone down though; there was still a search for her boyfriend, who was suspected of murdering her. Being in a desolate area really helped shelter us from a lot of the publicity. I knew that no matter what, I didn't want to use this connection for any sort of monetary or personal gain. I wanted to be respectful of everything her parents asked. I couldn't even begin to imagine what they were experiencing; I didn't want to add any level of stress to it.

My phone rang one day, and it was Nichole. She asked if I would come to Gabby's service, which was happening in a few days. I told her that I'd have to check with Kyle, and I would get back to her.

I knew I needed to go, but could I really leave Kyle with managing the family for a few days when he was about to start the night shift with Jed and Sandy at the harvest? That would be a lot to put on him.

After I hung up, I walked over to Kyle, who was standing outside with our friends by the campfire, and somehow, he knew exactly who called and what they asked.

"You know you have to go, right?" Kyle said. "I know," I replied.

Just then, Jessa said, "Jenn, we've got the kids. You need to go; we'll hold it down here."

With everyone in agreement, I bought my plane ticket, and before I knew it, Kyle was dropping me and my service dog Theodore off at the Grand Forks International Airport.

FOLLOWING MY YELLOW FEELING

After I'd made it to the La Quinta Inn & Suites the previous evening, I started today thinking that I was going to spend it in the hotel room, binge watching mindless TV.…

Then, suddenly, I was in Long Island, New York to attend a memorial service the following day, and I was feeling all sorts of overwhelm.

Truth be told, I wasn't confident in myself (especially after the debacle that was my travel day yesterday) to navigate around Long Island on my lonesome. Directions and me, well, we don't see eye to eye. I could get lost in a wet paper bag.…

After a call to my sister, she encouraged me to take life by the balls and just GO. Don't have a plan, just go from one thing to the next.

After deliberating with Theodore, my service dog, if this was the best course of action…I just decided to go for it…and man, I'm sure glad I did.

Once we left the room, we decided to take the short walk to Starbucks. I felt that if I started small and simple…it wouldn't be so bad.

The hint of crisp fall weather was in the air. It wasn't too cold, but it took the edge off being hot—literally the perfect temperature. Theodore's long ears floated in the wind, and we strolled to that infamous green Starbucks sign.

Once we got there, I was in line to order my black venti Veranda Blend with my spinach and artichoke egg bites when a man comes behind us and remarks on Theodore. He tells me that he is a well-trained service dog. I just smile and pleasantly say thank you and carry on with my order.

I decided that for every person who passed me, I would smile and say hello, making sure to ask how their day was. If nothing else today, I knew I wanted to be a bright spot and make people feel validated and seen.

Thinking that it might be fun, I would also ask a person at each place I was where I should go next. I explained to the barista what I was doing and asked her where I should go? Thinking for a moment, she paused and then said, "If you like shopping, you should go to Patchogue."

Once Theodore and I got seated, I looked up places to go. The first thing that crossed my mind was to go to a boutique; I'm a sucker for eccentric earrings. The first store that came up on my phone was named the Say More Boutique. Fitting, I suppose, because I was blessed with the gift of gab.

Once I ordered our Uber, it was time to load up and head to the next destination, Say More. When James came to pick me up, to say that I was nervous was a gross understatement. Just yesterday, I was turned down for a ride because of Theodore, and I was afraid for it to happen again.

Lucky for me, this is a serendipitous day! I was letting the universe guide me, and it wasn't going to guide me into any heartache. James, my Uber driver, was so wonderful! We talked the entire time he drove me to my destination. It was a delightful conversation and just made my heart so full.

Theodore and I said our goodbyes and stepped out of the car, onto the curb, right by Say More Boutique. Upon inspection, I noticed that it was closed. It was about 11:10 a.m., and it said it was supposed to open at 11:00. I knew it was okay because well, it's a serendipitous day!

I made the choice to come back in a few minutes, so Theodore and I headed off walking in another direction.

I came across the other boutique called Tell Your Tale. Once I saw this, I knew today would be filled with signs....

It was a quaint little place when we walked in. There were racks of clothes, jewelry, and earrings. Everything you'd expect a fun clothing boutique to be. I perused all the racks and ended up in the jewelry section (I end up at the jewelry section a lot). I saw these blue, round, flat-beaded, hoop earrings. They just stood out to me for being sturdy yet delicate. It was at that moment I knew they needed to come live with me.

I made small talk with the cashier, putting out as much good energy as I could. She was incredibly friendly and kind. She even remarked on how well behaved Theodore was. I thanked her for the earrings, and we went on our way. I had this feeling when I left: I felt yellow. Yellow, bright like the sun, or fresh-squeezed lemonade. Just a warm, happy feeling.

I thought to myself, "Okay, maybe there is something here on this serendipitous day...."

Theodore and I moseyed back to Say More Boutique, fresh with this yellow feeling.

As soon as we walked in the door, my heart couldn't help but smile. It was this indescribable energy that filled my heart with joy. The aroma was light and airy, like a bouquet of freshly picked daisies. The boutique was bright and beautiful, very minimalistic with the clothing.

A cheerful girl sat behind the desk and smiled as I walked in. I asked her how her day was, and she replied by asking about mine. Something inside told me to keep talking, asking where I should go next.

I started by asking what her name was, and she replied, "It's Jenn, what's yours?"

I said, "What?! My name is Jenn with two Ns!" She exclaimed, "Me too!"

I knew I was in the right place.

She began to tell me about many different places, but the one that resonated with me was Davis Park. It was electric. It was that same feeling I had at each place I went to before. She told me that I should catch the ferry to Fire Island; oddly enough, Fire Island didn't have that electric feeling. Hmmm. Weird....

As I was browsing the boutique, I came across these light wooden basket-weave earrings. I love to collect earrings from places that I go to, so I instantly knew these were coming home with me.

As I went to check out, we continued to have casual conversation. Mostly talking about Long Island and what I should do in the short time I'm there.

I took out my debit card and handed it to her, so that I could pay for my darling little earrings.

Suddenly, she says something that stops me in my tracks.

"Bethune. Bethune? You're HER. Oh, my god. You found that video. You're a hero. Thank you so much! This town owes you so much!" She gushed.

I think it's important to note that I don't see myself as a hero. I am just someone who did the right thing, that's all.

She asks if she can give me a hug, and of course, I absolutely welcome it! (This entire experience has taught me to appreciate the touch of other humans and how truly calming it can be.)

We said our goodbyes, and I was on my way, on to the best serendipitous location.

I let the electric feeling be my guide. I didn't know where it came from, but I just knew in my gut that it wouldn't let me down. I pulled my phone out to catch an Uber, but that electric feeling told me to put it away and just keep walking; there was something I needed to see....

The town was so quaint and cute! Everything that you'd imagine a small town in the movies to be. Shoppers were going in and out of stores, patrons were enjoying a delicious lunch on the restaurant patios...and then I saw it.

There were Boy Scouts raising money by selling popcorn up on the right, in an alleyway. They were wearing orange handkerchiefs to signify that they were Tiger Cubs. They couldn't have been more than six or seven years old.

Now I have to tell you this piece of crucial information. Ethan was a Tiger Cub, and his handkerchief was orange too. He was buried in his Boy Scout uniform.

Crazy, right? Electric feeling-three, Jenn-zero.

I didn't have any cash, but I did spot an ATM across the street. I made a bee line to the cash dispenser, and that electric feeling came buzzing back....

When it prompted time to select a cash amount, the feeling kept telling me to select $200....

Feeling in the serendipitous spirit, I listened.

I grabbed my freshly dispensed cash and headed back over to the boys. I gave them a twenty-dollar bill for their jar and bebopped back on our way.

I thought I needed to grab an Uber because my destination being Davis Park, it would have been a half hour walk. Before I knew it, the old electric feeling was back, and it was nudging me to put my phone away. Keep walking.

This electric feeling is starting to have an excellent track record....

As I kept walking past the remainder of the stores on the main drag of the town, the buildings were becoming more spread apart instead of the storefronts being the same structure. Teenagers with bright neon-colored poster board were waving cars down to come to their car wash.

Upon further inspection, I saw they were raising money for their team to go to a major league game. Theodore and I crossed the street and headed down to where there was a makeshift cash register with flyers, empty containers of cream cheese, and slices of bagels everywhere. My first thought was that teenage boys are total garbage disposals, and they can't get enough food....

Then, I tracked one of the teens down and donated another twenty-dollar bill for the cause and headed out on my way.

I kept walking down this side road, the landscape started to become more housing than business, and I decided it was best to call that Uber now, and (finally) the electric feeling didn't disagree with me.

Within five minutes, my driver pulled up. Theodore and I hopped into the backseat, putting him in a "down stay" position on the floor.

My driver was very nice, and we made small talk the entire time. It was a short ride, only about six minutes, but as we approached our destination, E (can we just shorten *electric feeling* at this point? Great, thanks) came back and gave me the urge to give my driver one of the twenty-dollar bills. So, I did.

When I got out, the ferry to Fire Island was CLOSED. Well, damn.

The driver asked me if I was sure he wanted him to leave me in a mostly deserted parking lot. I replied, "Oh, totally, I'll be fine. Have a great day!"

As I expected, E came back and told me to walk around down by the shoreline. Seeing as how E has had a pretty good track record so far, I heeded its nudging.

As I walked through the deserted parking lot, I noticed a small lighthouse, and my steps got quicker the more in focus the lighthouse became. Once I made it to the shore, there was a walkway lined with silver metal railing leading straight up to the mostly white tiny lighthouse.

This wasn't the type of lighthouse that you could walk into; in fact, the metal rail prevented you from even getting to it. My best guess is that it was just used for boats coming into the small harbor.

In that moment, my Apple Watch buzzed, alerting me to "do one minute of deep breathing."

E popped back up and urged me to listen to Siri, and I closed my eyes as I began to inhale deeply through my nose.

I don't know what it is about the crisp salt water air that just cleanses your soul, but it's incredibly refreshing. I let out a long, slow, and releasing sigh of an exhale. It was in that moment that I let everything go.…

Ten years of grief from losing Ethan.

Finding the van footage.

Being strong for Gabby's memorial.

The anxiety of traveling by myself and navigating a large city.

Flying on planes.

Theodore performing all weekend.

And so many past traumas. The deeper breaths I took, the more I let go. I let go of the things I couldn't control. I let go of all my failures. I let go of all my shortcomings. I let it ALL go.

I breathed in that misty salt air and let it cleanse my entire soul.

I was free. I opened my eyes, awakened from what felt like a deep sleep of heavy emotional burdens.

I gave one final exhale, and as I turned around, what looked like a gray-haired father and his adult son were walking up to the end of the path, pushing their bikes.

Knowing that in the beginning of the day, I set out to smile and talk to each person I came across, that's exactly what I did.

I smiled, said hello, and asked how they were doing today. As soon as the last word left my lips, Dad's face lit up. He looked shocked that someone would take the time to acknowledge their existence.

He joyfully replied, "Oh, hi! We are good; how about yourself?"

I casually said, "I am great. Have an amazing day!" and strolled back down the concrete walkway.

Instead of going back to catch an Uber, E popped back up and nudged me to go right and walk along the dock next to the water, listening to the gurgling sounds crashing on the pylons of the dock.

The salty sea air continued to cleanse my soul, bringing me peace throughout my body. I thought of Gabby and how she brought us here. My thoughts went to Ethan and how I never truly grieved when I lost him.

Theodore and I took a seat on the edge of the dock, my feet dangling a foot or so from the crashing water. While sitting there, I realized that I was finally able to let it go. I was able to know that Ethan was with Gabby, and he was at peace.

Once I had felt that I let everything go and my soul was at rest, it was time to get up and get to the rest of this beautiful day.

Theodore and I made our way back to where the driver had dropped us off, and I pulled out my phone, not to call an Uber, but to look up where I should eat. The first restaurant that popped up was right there, about a hundred yards away at the marina. E approved, and off we went.

When I walked up, I noticed it was an open-air restaurant in the middle and a separate tiki bar on the left. Making a quick decision, I went left to sit at the bar. Something just told me that this was where I needed to be.

The bar was mostly empty except for one patron named Steve and the bartender. Once I sat down and put Theodore in a down stay, I ordered my food: a crispy Caesar salad accompanied by Tito's and club soda with a lime.

I chatted with Steve and our bartender for a good twenty minutes before a group of people came up, dressed in fancier attire. They ordered some drinks in a hurry. They explained the ferry was shut down because there was a private wedding on Fire Island that they were attending. They arrived early, so they came to the bar.

It was then that a news headline came on the TV above the bar. It was about a missing girl, Gabby Petito who was on a van trip with her boyfriend and was found murdered. Which, coincidentally, was the reason I was in Long Island all along. There was a vlogging family that found footage of Gabby's missing van that led the FBI to finding Gabby's body.

We were that family.

Gabby's mom, Nichole, asked me to come. At that time, the rest of my family wasn't able to attend because of previous commitments they had. This was something that I knew I needed to do despite being utterly terrified to travel alone without my family and having PTSD.

So here I was, sitting at a bar at Davis Park on Long Island, New York with my service dog, having a serendipitous day, preparing to go to a funeral the next day when I heard from the wedding guests right behind my back....

"Oh, wow. That's Gabby. I was her music teacher in the fifth grade. She was so talented, and I really enjoyed having her in my class. It's so tragic what happened."

I smiled. Gabby just introduced me to her teacher, and I was honored. Knowing it wasn't about me, I simply listened. Feeling the need to observe instead of insert myself, I kept facing away from them and wrapped up in eating my salad. The wedding goers paid their tabs and went about their way.

Earlier, I had made the other Jenn with 2 Ns promise she wouldn't tell anyone I was here. It was truly important to me for nobody to know who I am, or why I was here. This trip wasn't about me; it was about being there to support Nichole, another momma who lost her baby in a tragic way. I did everything I could to stay incognito.

After the wedding guests departed for their exclusive ferry, I asked Steve where I should go next on my serendipitous day. His response was immediate. "Ya gotta go to Montauk! It's gorgeous out there. Just hop the train around the corner, and it'll take ya straight there!"

I smiled because it always brought me joy to hear a New York accent. It was actually Steve's retirement day, so he was especially energetic, and it warmed my heart knowing he finally felt free, too.

As I was leaving, I went to pay my tab, and the bartender told me that Steve paid for me on his way out. As if my heart couldn't be any fuller! What a gem that Steve was! Getting to connect with people and learn more about their lives is one of my utmost favorite experiences to have.

Our good buddy Electric Feeling was back and nudged me to leave two twenty-dollar bills on the counter for my bartender. Theodore and I trotted off to the train.

It's important to mention at this point in my life, I had never ridden a train by myself. This would be a first for me, and to say I was anxious is a gross understatement.

Still, I knew today wasn't going to let me down, and I picked up my spirits and walked up onto the platform to discover…all the trains going to Montauk were done for the day.

Well, crap. What do I do now?

As expected, the Universe always provides when I'm living in alignment with my highest good. I turned to my left and saw a tall older gentleman with thinning hair and a Members Only jacket.

"Hey, where are you headed, ma'am? Are you okay?" He asked.

Me being me, I went into the synopsis of my day, and once I explained the serendipitous part, I asked him where I should go next.

"That is so cool!" He exclaimed. "Okay. You've gotta take the train up to Babylon. I think you'll really enjoy it there."

The train was just pulling into the station, and we said our goodbyes as Theodore and I hopped on board.

"This sure was a thrill," I thought to myself. "I am here, in Long Island, on a freaking train, by myself!!" Proud was the understatement of the year. A huge smile spread across my face as I gazed out of the window.

The train whizzed by the scenery of nestled together houses and crowded town streets.

Before I knew it, we reached my stop. Theodore and I got up and walked out onto the platform, beaming with adventure and excitement.

Just as I was unsure of where to go, E came back in, and I felt like going to the left.

We crossed the street out of the train station, and I noticed that Babylon wasn't very busy or crowded. It was in fact, empty. Even though it was quiet, I wasn't scared. Oddly enough I was immensely calm.

My gaze caught a homeless man sitting in a corner, tucked next to a brick wall. I reached into my pocket and grabbed some money. At the time, I didn't even know how much, and I just handed it to him. I told him that I hope he had a really great day and went about my way.

It didn't matter to me what his intentions with it were; what mattered was that he needed it more than I did, and I had it to give.

I'd been walking down a tree-lined street with businesses and houses mixed in together. Each town had its own charm, and this one was no different. It had gotten busier in this area, which looked very affluent.

My electric feeling came in, and I glanced at the sign above me....

Pandemonium Boutique, it read. I immediately knew I needed to go inside.

I pushed open the old wood door with a huge glass window, and I discovered a quaint little shop with clothes on every wall. In the middle were beautifully decorated tables mixed in with various tops, pants, and accessories.

My eyes met the woman working there, and I smiled.

She asked me if I was looking for anything in particular, and I went in to explain my serendipitous day and how I got here. It was then that I had an idea....

I asked her if she would be up for curating an outfit for me to wear, anything she thought that I needed in my closet. Whatever she picked out, I'd made up in my mind that I was buying.

In this stage of my fashion journey, I was looking for a comfy lounge suit thing. You know, kind of like a jogger pants on the bottom, sweatshirt-y thing on top? Well, because I'm fun sized, as I say for being five-foot-two, clothes don't always fit me like they fit average-height folks. I'd been searching for this dream outfit of mine for months—to no avail.

Wouldn't you know what I got handed in my dressing room?

The absolute perfect jogger set thing. It was literally exactly what I had envisioned in my head. The real test was, of course, if it was actually going to fit me.

This was a serendipitous day, y'all, you know it's going to fit.

And it did, like a perfect glove. I even got an outfit to wear for the memorial service the following day.

I said my goodbyes to Pandemonium, and as I was walking out the door, I lifted my bag to get a closer look of the drawing she drew on it…

It was a sunflower.

"Of course it is," I said to myself with a big grin. Sunflowers were Ethan's (and Gabby's) favorite flower. It was fitting for a perfect day.

At that moment, I felt it was time to go home; however, the universe wasn't done just yet.

A notification popped on my Apple Watch. Gabby's mom Nichole texted me. I was going to be meeting her at some point in the day; we just didn't know when. I fully understood and wanted to be flexible and accommodate whatever time was best for her. Even if I didn't get to see her at all, I was happy just to be there to support good energy.

In the text, she said she would be at my hotel in about thirty to forty-five minutes. I needed to get back ASAP!

Standing under a big clock tower on the corner of the street, I had my phone out, just finishing calling my Uber when I noticed an elderly gentleman who was having a difficult time crossing the street. I walked over to him as he reached the side I was on and asked him if he was okay.

He began to talk about his health issues and how he has been feeling really down lately. I smiled and inquisitively asked, "How does someone who only looks like he is about twenty-eight have these problems?!?"

A big grin spread from ear to ear on his face, and he chuckled.

"What's your name kid?" He asked.

"I'm Jenn. What's yours?"

"Hi, Jenn. I'm John. It's nice to meet you. You really have made my day, and I sure needed this."

I talked to him about my serendipitous day and how we lived in a bus with our kids traveling around the country. He listened in amazement, making me feel so seen and heard.

As we said our goodbyes, my Uber pulled up, and I knew it was time to go.

On the ride back to the La Quinta Inn & Suites, my Uber driver and I chatted mostly about his son and how much he loved spending time with him. Most recently they loved to go and get ice cream every day he got to pick him up from school.

My thoughts went back to when I would pick Ethan up from school and head to Walt Disney World for the day. He'd would be so happy and excited to see me, just as I was to see him. I began to feel bright and yellow, much like I did earlier today at the lighthouse. I was grateful for my driver sharing his life with me, and I got to experience a beautiful memory of mine.

When we arrived at the hotel, I handed him the rest of the money in my pocket, and I told him to take his son out for ice cream in memory of mine. I thanked him for our ride together, and I shut the door; Theodore and I headed up to our room to change.

Shortly after I put on my new perfect jogging suit thing, I got a text from Nichole. She was here.

My heart started to race as I crossed the lobby, out the front doors.

I came around a tall bush as Nichole was stepping onto the curb from the parking lot, and we rushed towards each other and immediately embraced. Everything we needed to say to each other was exchanged in energy.

We didn't have much time, but I was just grateful for the time I did get to have with her and Tara, Gabby's stepmom.

I felt the need to tell them about my serendipitous day and my yellow feeling. When I finished the tale of my magical day, Nichole placed a little glass heart in my hand. It was mixed colors with some clear. Someone had melted glass down and formed them into these little hearts. They made them for Nichole to give out to special people, and she gave this one to me. Would you like to take a guess as to what colors it was?

It was a mix of yellows.

Of course it was yellows; I couldn't help but grin. As I held it in my hand, so many pieces of the shattered glass that was my heart, melted back together, just like this heart.

I said my goodbyes to Nichole, letting her know I'd be there tomorrow. I went back up to my room with Theodore and tried to soak in what that day meant to me.

✋ REST STOP #2
SEEK SILENCE

Seek Silence by putting your phone on DND for fifteen minutes a day.

Throughout the years on my healing journey, I've discovered that the best way to get answers to the queries you've been asking is to ask yourself.

As I was standing at that lighthouse on Long Island, I listened to that nudge to be still and breathe while soaking in the silence.

Often, we think that the validation we need in our lives comes from people around us. Society has taught us to seek others for that validation because we certainly shouldn't know ourselves, and we need to find the answers elsewhere.

I've found that is one huge misconception. The only true validation we need is from within ourselves. Once we feel valid, we can release so much grief and other heavy emotions like I did at the lighthouse.

In order to find that validation, we have to go within. To do that, we must remove as many outside distractions as we can.

Take a moment and think about your phone. Try and recall how often your phone is in your hand. When you first wake up. While you're eating breakfast. On the road to work. On every break at work. On the road back home. While you're cooking dinner. While you're cleaning. Sometimes when you shower. While you're lying in bed. Do you see a recurring theme here?

There aren't many times in a day that people are without this little box attached to their body.

If it's with you all the time, when do you silence the outside noise and have quiet time to yourself?

When you're carrying a phone constantly, you lose the ability to think for yourself. All the answers reside in Google. Need to find Chinese food? Look on Yelp. Gotta get new shoes? Open up Amazon. Need to see what your friend's doing? Tap open Instagram.

We are so distracted by all the things all the time that we forget to live in this moment. The past makes us feel guilty; the future makes us feel anxious. With the ability to sit in silence, you feel calm in the present.

It seems unbelievable, but there are more than six billion cell phone users across the globe. Six billion. That's a lot of little communication boxes being carried around. That's also a lot of people not taking breaks from them to get some clarity.

By no means am I saying to ditch the phone all together. They often come in handy, especially when you're on the road.

But, it's all in how you use them. Just like with anything in life, moderation and discernment is the key.

How It Goes

Find a time in your day that you want dedicated to seeking silence. It doesn't have to be the same time, just whenever you're able to fit in fifteen minutes to just sit alone and focus on you.

You can do this in your parked car during lunch break. Sitting on a blanket under a tree in a park. Locking yourself in your bathroom at your house with a sign on the door saying, "Do not Disturb."

Wherever you can do it, make it happen. The location isn't as important as the act of actually doing it.

As far as people being able to reach you, I have a list of emergency contacts that ring through do not disturb. The people who matter the most can reach me within that fifteen minutes if they need to.

Now, relax your jaw and loosen your shoulders. I want you to take a deep breath, slowly inhaling through your nose for *one, two, three, four, five* seconds. Pause for one second, letting yourself float in the stillness.

Put your lips together in a kiss and exhale slowly through your mouth for *five, four, three, two, one.*

Repeat these two more times. I'll wait for you here ;-).

How do you feel? Are you able to notice a little bit of the overwhelming loosening? The more often you seek silence, put your phone on do not disturb, and get uncomfortable in the quiet, the longer that golden feeling of calm stays, and releasing the subconscious trauma tied in the heavy emotions can happen.

Pausing for a moment and taking in my entire journey thus far, every single day, each second in time, has made me who I am right now. Without taking these moments, I may not have become me.

While my whole journey and everything that happens in it is meaningful, some lessons have more significance to them, and you feel more deeply.

The most valuable thing I have learned is that my journey is entirely individual and unique to me. My journey and finding true happiness and contentment is completely up to me. Not my circumstances. Not my family. Not my location. Not even the choices I've made in the past. My future journey is up to my present self to decide.

It was a late May day in Newport, Oregon in the spring of 2022, and we'd just pulled into a state park for a week's stay. It had been a super rainy and dreary day, which meant Kyle had to be very diligent with paying attention to driving the bus. I was following behind in our not-yet-built-out campervan, and my PTSD made me exhausted. We had gotten into an argument, and I headed out for a walk in the Oregon misty and damp woods.

Kyle is a very to-himself kind of person and forgets about others sometimes. It was a rough day of driving and I was following behind him driving our van. We have a protocol where we make sure I have directions before we pull off. On this particular day, Kyle would forget to make sure I had the coordinates before turning into traffic. This would cause my panic to surge and I'd have to do some deep breathing with some kind words to my inner self that I could do this.

When we got parked, it was probably the wrong time to mention it to Kyle, but my frustration was right under the surface and my ego wanted to feel valid.

Me voicing what I'd like to do better next time, triggered Kyle and his eyes went soulless.

On my walk, the trees were so green, I'd never seen this deep bright of a hue before. I kept walking, my mind continuing to race. I was furious and frazzled. So discombobulated in fact, that I'd forgotten my phone back on the bus. I remembered about a mile in, and I didn't feel like going back; I was too far gone, and I trudged on.

I wasn't even aware what this state park had until I ended up on a seaside cliff of tall swaying grass, overlooking the sea. "Whoa. This was breathtaking," I remember gasping out loud. I found a nice spot on the edge, overlooking the sandy beach below.

The sky was gray and hazy as I closed my eyes and laid backward onto the grass, breathing in the cool salty air.

I felt my heart rate slowly go down, and the overwhelming cyclone in my mind went away. I began to ask myself questions about why I was mad at Kyle, and that led me to ask deeper questions about who I was and who I wanted to be.

For three hours, I lay in that cozy tall grass asking questions and actually receiving answers to the things I had been desperately wanting to know. On my walk back, I'd felt more refreshed and alive than I'd ever felt before.

I was just present in the moment, listening to the orchestra of sounds around me, and realizing how good it made my entire self and body feel.

Being present in the moment. What a wild experience that was!

Looking back, that day was crucial to me in choosing to use nature to heal my trauma. Now, I've incorporated that growing opportunity into my daily routine. I call it observing the moment.

✋ REST STOP #3
OBSERVE THE MOMENT

I put my phone on "Do not Disturb," and I go out in nature for at least fifteen minutes. I am searching for a spot where I can see the sky with the clouds passing by.

It could be sitting under a tree on a blanket, perhaps on a park bench, or even at an outdoor city cafe with plants on the patio.

I sit in silence and focus on my breathing. I listen to the wind rustle the leaves. I hear the birds singing a melody to their neighbors. Laughter erupts as I see a mom push her daughter on the swing. When disrupting thoughts come into my mind, I shift my focus back to my breathing and focus my eyes on the clouds above me.

I observe them floating gingerly through the bright blue sunny sky. I watch as they transform shapes and the breeze blows them out of my view.

I notice a squirrel is running down from the tree, gathering acorns to store in its secret spot. The ants are marching across the sidewalk with food to bring back to their colony. Grandpa is playing catch with his grandchildren, whose hearts are full.

By taking this time daily for as brief a time as fifteen minutes, life slows down. The overwhelm has a chance to settle, and I can catch my breath. By the end of my session, I feel balanced and clear, grateful for that little bit of pure peace in my day.

In observing the moment, I cannot insert myself into others' lives and stay present in my own.

LETTING GO OF THE NEED TO BE LIKED

The summer of 2022, coming up on a year after we found the footage, we were building a campervan in rural Washington state, about an hour east of Spokane in a town called Cusick. Our friends, Jed and Sandy, put their van lives on hold to help us build it.

On this particular day, we were teaching our kids fractions by using the tape measure and hands-on building. We made a video about this lesson, and it spread like wildfire. Before we knew it, we had five videos getting hundreds of millions of views on four social media platforms. The trolls came out in droves, commenting.

The previous summer, finding footage that helped the FBI bring someone's remains home had made international news, and of course there were some negative responses, so we thought we were used to it. What was happening now, however, would throw me into a spiral of self-discovery and shadow work that tore apart my ego and self-identity.

When I say "go into my shadow," what I am doing is sitting in silence within myself after I have a trigger or a big heavy emotion come up. I don't push it away; I don't fight it. I simply let it be there. I sit in it. I allow myself to feel it without being consumed by it. I accept that I was triggered, or I'd had a big reactive emotion, and I gently remind myself that I am a human who has a range of emotions. I validate the pain I'm feeling by letting it take its space for a moment.

Sitting in my shadow is where I've found that peace begins.

I take the heavy emotion I am feeling, and I trace it back to where it came from. I shift my focus to the imagining that comes up in my mind's eye. When one appears, I follow it, allowing it to show me my real-life memory of an event where trauma occurred.

As I see myself at that moment in my mind's eye, I visualize giving my then self a much-needed hug. I tell my past self it wasn't my fault, and I am enough just as I am. The big emotions of that past memory begin to dissipate as I recognize that person involved with me was doing the best they could with those current capabilities they had. They were acting out of their unhealed trauma towards me, having no idea what they were doing.

This doesn't excuse what they did; however, it allows me to see them for who they are, releasing me from continuing to carrying those heavy emotions around the memory.

I genuinely forgive them, for they knew not what they were doing. I also forgive myself for anything I'd done to hurt them, having the knowledge that we are all doing our best we can in every moment. If we are on our conscious healing journey, we make a better choice when that scenario comes around again. When we learn from our trauma, we make better choices in the future.

Whenever I am triggered by someone or something, I do that practice of shadow work. Each time I work through the trigger when I am triggered, I can find my calm more quickly. That particular big emotion needed to be seen, felt, heard, and validated in order to be released. What I noticed over time when I practiced this regularly was that my major triggers became less and less frequent. Doing this also helped me to discover that I could begin to find my calm in the chaos.

Now in my healing journey, I'm able to do this shadow work within a few seconds after being triggered. In doing my shadow work to heal and release trauma, I've discovered awareness and genuine inner peace.

When I say, "go into my shadow," what I am doing is sitting in silence within myself after I have a trigger or a big heavy emotion come up. I don't push it away; I don't fight it. I simply let it be there. I sit in it. I allow myself to feel it without being consumed by it. I accept that I was triggered or I'd had a really big reactive emotion and I gently remind myself that I am a human that has a range of emotion. I validate the pain I'm feeling, by letting it take its space for a moment.

Sitting in my shadow is where I've found that peace begins.

I take the heavy emotion I am feeling and I trace it back to where it came from. I shift my focus to the imagining that comes up in my mind's eye. When one appears, I follow it, allowing it to show me my real-life memory of an event where trauma occurred.

As I see myself at that moment in my mind's eye, I visualize giving my then self a much-needed hug. I tell my past self it wasn't my fault and I am enough just as I am. The big emotions of that past memory begin to dissipate as I recognize that person involved with me was doing the best they could with those current capabilities they had. They were acting out of their unhealed trauma towards me, having no idea what they were doing.

This doesn't excuse what they did, however it allows me to see them for who they are, releasing me from continuing to carrying those heavy emotions around the memory.

Back at the van build, millions and millions of people were giving me their opinions. Some great. Some good. Some bad. And some...they were a new level of disgusting. We got a lot of people who were upset. Some of the comments even saying I should be "put to death for the way [I] abuse my children." We also got so many positive words of praise and love, but the number of broken people hurling their pent-up anger and heavy emotions at us began to overshadow the good.

That type of criticism, in front of millions of people, had my sense of self crumbling. I didn't even know who I was anymore or who even I wanted to be. Still, being thrown in front of that firing squad is one of the things I am most grateful for in life. It ripped away who I thought I was and created space for me to choose who I now wanted to be.

Having so many people give you their perspective about who you are as a person at once was soul shattering. I knew I wasn't who they were saying I was. They are getting a small clip of our lives from a fifteen-second video and making snap assumptions from it.

Our purpose in making our videos was to show others that an alternative lifestyle with your family was not only possible, but you could thrive doing it. This really was a huge catalyst of seeing just how many people do, act, and say things out of their emotion caused by their unhealed trauma.

It was during this firing squad of hatefulness and negative energy where I found empathy for the trolls.

In Cusick, where we were building our campervan, it was a desolate small northwestern Washington state town. The town may have been small, but the surroundings were BIG! Across from our campground there was a beautiful, slow-moving clear river and a backdrop of stunning snowcapped mountain views.

I spent a lot of free time sitting by the river and being with myself after all the bombardment of despicable comments. I released so much resentment and hate I had triggered in me toward them. With some shadow work, I discovered they represented my mother and her constant criticism of everything I ever did. Nothing I did was ever right or good enough in her eyes. If I tried to advocate for myself with her, she would beat me down with her perspective and how wrong I was. I was reliving that in this cycle, just in the form of very hurting people making hundreds of thousands of comments online.

The stillness of the river and the soaring eagles high above made for such a beautiful energy of peace.

Even though we were getting utterly slammed with hate, I was able to use nature to help me explore my shadow.

Another key I feel to unlocking part of yourself and who you're meant to be is simple: Nature.

Living in a bus and traveling the country, we have been to some of the most incredible and breathtaking landscapes you could ever imagine. Zion. Yellowstone. The Tetons. Grand Canyon. The Rockies. Lake Superior. And so many more like them. The moments in nature that healed my soul, however, were deep in the woods or on Long Island at a lighthouse. It was the moments that I felt that were the ones that I created space for nature to touch my soul.

THE AD*VAN*TURE OF OUR LIVES

It was July 4, and the fireworks display was erupting across the river at the Native American Reservation in Cusick, Washington. Jed, Sandy, Kyle, and the kids were watching in amazement bursts of gold, green, and blue while I was in the bus bathroom from eating too much dairy at our feast earlier in the evening.

Tomorrow was the day that we'd be embarking on a really big adventure. Our bus, Blue Betty, was going to be getting a kitchen and bunk remodel down in Arizona as we traveled in our newly built campervan with Sandy and Jed.

We spent the previous five and a half weeks with our buddies Jed and Sandy, who put their lives on hold to help us build our campervan Bodhi. This campervan was built to hold nine living things: Kyle, me, our kids, and four dogs. It was like playing human Tetris. There's an entire build series and a plethora of adVANtures on our YouTube channel if you want to see how we did it. Video really is the only way to describe the coziness, lol. Ready or not, we would be spending eight to twelve weeks traveling during the summer in our new van while Blue Betty was away getting her remodel.

The plan was that Kyle and our youngest son Eli would drive the bus down to Arizona, drop it off with Michael, then both of them would fly to meet us near Seattle in the van. I would take Ben, Molly, and all four dogs with me, while Jed and Sandy traveled with in their van.

It was going to be a wild adVANture…for all of us.

BODHI: SPIRITUAL AWAKENING OR ENLIGHTENMENT

Social media is a lot for anyone, especially a content creator. It can give you the highest feeling of the high and the lowest feeling of the low, sometimes in the span of twenty minutes.

Creating content is truly a form of art. After all, it comes straight from your soul. When you pour your heart and soul into something, you can get quite attached to it.

Putting so much of yourself into something can be a blessing…and a curse. When people pour love right back into you, it's one of the most incredible feelings you can experience. But, if they pour hate, and if you let it bother you, the hate starts to seep into your self-identity.

Compound all of that with the unattainable algorithm, which attempts to dictate your every life decision…and well, then the burnout becomes inherently real.

Social media isn't a job that you can truly "clock out" of. If we allow it to, our phones become stuck to our noses, and social media wants to be the only thing you're eating, sleeping, and breathing. When you're living in creating content, it becomes quite difficult to simply "unplug."

This is why taking a social media hiatus is imperative to your mental health. You need to disconnect with technology in order to reconnect with yourself.

At this point, we'd been in the van together for about six weeks, and we hadn't been doing well mentally; in fact, we had been struggling a great deal. Trying to manage our social media, be parents, tend to our relationship, make sure our dogs got enough exercise, having to move every night, all in 120 square feet was really burning the candle at every end.

That burnout? It was becoming VERY real. I knew that we needed to pause and catch our breath before we exploded. We stopped posting long form videos and just made short form. Trying to show all the aspects of vanlife as a family while trying to live it.

At first, when we took our break, we thought the sole cause for our mental health decline was Bodhi, our van....

...but in all honesty, the van was another catalyst to growth. If you want rapid growth in a short amount of time, squeeze your entire family and pets into a teeny tiny camper with nowhere else to stay for three months.

Although I wouldn't recommend doing it if you haven't begun your mental health journey already. Having that much rapid growth can be a disaster if you don't have a toolbox full of mental health instruments to pull out and use.

But alas, I digress…

During this stage on our mental health path, Kyle was working through a lot of problems, mainly with parenting and how to be more kind and loving with the kids. My energy at the time was being focused on supporting Kyle in his moments of depression rather than becoming frustrated that he was having them.

We're developing and building all these skills, but they were being thrust into a combustion chamber that came in the form of a tiny van. Here's the thing though: We needed it to implode in order to rebuild. We truly required that rapid jumpstart, so we could see that we needed to pause, breathe, and evaluate what was going on.

Kyle was adamant we couldn't afford to take a break from social media, and I was just as unwavering in the fact that we couldn't afford NOT to take one.

We needed to simply exist in nature, get grounded in who we are, reconnect with our kids, and we did it by laying down all of our technology and really soaking in the world around us.

After an exhausting three days of searching for a boondocking spot, we came across the perfect one. It was by a lake with just enough cell service to be able to call someone if we had an emergency.

The beauty of this majestic place was remarkable! It looked as though we were staying inside an incredible Bob Ross painting. The reflection of the trees on the still glass lake, the bee's wings buzzing and dashing around us, the soft chirps of the finches in the trees above.

Loose dirt was covering the ground. As the dogs ran by, it created dust clouds, carried off by a cool breeze, then gingerly caressed our faces as it passed by. Eli, our youngest, dubbed that "dog smoke."

At times, golden rays of the sun would peek through the canopy of trees. Our kids' smiles lit up as they chased each other, illuminated by the beams of the sun, dancing amongst the leaves.

The dogs would plop down in the dirt to bathe in the warmth of that big glowing orb while Kyle and I relaxed in the hammocks, nestled in the cool shade of the towering Douglas firs.

At one point, during this time in our heaven on earth, I stood upon a flat rock, letting my hands fall by my sides while lifting my head toward the warm sunshine and closing my eyes. All of a sudden, the breeze picked up speed and before I knew it, my arms were outstretched as far wide as they could go. It's as if I was soaring like the wild eagle above me.

The gale of wind kept coming, blowing right through my body, relieving me of the negative energy I'd accumulated over the last few months. I felt as if I was being bathed in a yellow, warm, and glowing sphere, feeling safe, valid, and loved.

The wind began to subside. I knew my time in this beautiful golden sphere was ending. I took one last deep inhale and opened my eyes....

My entire body and mind felt at peace and weightless. As I exhaled, my anxiety and depression were dissipating, leaving behind an immense sense of freedom, much like what I experienced on Long Island at the lighthouse.

I believe when you have these moments, it's a similar feeling to "leveling up" in your spiritual journey on earth. We must endure hard times in order to grow onto the next level and have gratitude for the calm moments in life.

While we still had a few weeks left in the van before the bus was ready, we have adapted new feelings toward Bodhi. We were appreciative and grateful for the opportunity to create unique memories with our little family. It would be such a shame to spend this time we were given being angry, resentful, and depressed.

Instead, we planned to soak it all in, every single giggle, happy accident, and tender loving moment we can. After all, we are only here on earth for a limited period of time. If you really think about it, why would we want to spend that time being anything other than grateful and balanced?

OUR SAVINGS IS GONE

We had a lot of growing opportunities in that summer VANcation home of ours. This next one hit us hard though.

Nearing the end of our van trip, we got a call that our property manager, who lived on our multi-unit property and took care of everything, had unexpectedly died. Kyle took this really hard because Roger was more than an employee; he was a true friend.

This meant we had to fly back to Florida, get things situated, then continue our travels. While we were there, we located a new property manager, got things settled, and came back to Bodhi, our van we left in Idaho at the time.

By October of 2022, we had picked up our bus from her gorgeous remodel, moved in, and were now dry camping with eighty-eight other families at the Albuquerque International Balloon Fiesta.

We got a call from our property manager saying that things had gone from bad to worse. Six of the eight tenants were refusing to pay their rent because they didn't like the new system we had to put in because they didn't like the property management company's policies that Roger, our last manager, didn't have.

By the time we were able to get those six tenants out, it had been nine months without the income we normally had. We had to drain our savings to repair six units because of all the damage left by the tenants. We had just spent some of our savings building the van and doing our remodel to our bus. Our social media wasn't doing that well and neither was our mental health, especially after coming straight out of the twelve-week adVANture.

We had to drive all the way from New Mexico, cancel our Baja Mexico plans, and spend the entire winter in Florida at Kyle's parents' farm, right where our highway to happy began.

Somehow, Kyle was able to secure a loan to be able to complete the repairs, so we could get the property on the market and sold. We knew our season of owning this property was coming to an end, and we were okay with that.

DOLLY-FREAKING-PARTON?!

We had spent the winter busting our you-know-whats to remodel the property ourselves, saving as much money as we could. By the time May came, we had all the units repaired and rented out, and thankfully we were collecting an income once again.

Because we had some cash flow, and life was balancing out again, it was time to leave Florida and get back to traveling after being stationary and broke for six months. We listed the property for sale and said our goodbyes to family; we were off again!

It wasn't long before we realized that we were in a new season of travel, too. We didn't have the big buffer of our savings anymore if something big happened; we knew we needed to be cautious with spending.

One day in mid-July, we were in the beautiful state of Michigan near Detroit when I got a call from a friend. She asked me if I wanted to interview for an upcoming reality family game show. She had a cool opportunity and thought it would be a great adventure for us.

Five families competing in and around Pigeon Forge, Tennessee doing various activities like a pancake-stacking challenge sounded like a blast! They were paying us, and we got to be on a family game show? Seven-year-old Jenn was pretty stinking excited and so was the rest of our family.

The best part of all? We would get to meet one of my idols, Dolly freaking Parton.

It was 7 a.m., and the sky was gray and drizzly in Pigeon Forge, Tennessee. We were up second in the zorb ball relay race. This was the first of the five competitions in the Pigeon Forge Family Challenge, and here I was staring down a gigantic plastic ball at the other end of what felt like a football field. This zorb ball, as it's called, was filled with two of my children sloshing in water, ready to be pushed by Kyle down to me.

Just a week earlier we were in the very upper west part in the Upper Peninsula of Michigan in a town called Houghton. It was originally known for mining copper, but we were there at an off-grid camping spot we stumbled upon called Perrault Lake.

At this lake, we were camping in our bus with our friends Delmara, Tom, Clarie, and Matt as well as all of our kids. This lake was absolutely picturesque. It seemed like a little cove with a forested walking trail bordering the lake's perimeter.

We'd spend nights sharing meals and having heartfelt conversations at night around the campfire and paddle boarding together by day. Even though we were still struggling month to month financially, we found wealth in the love we shared with our friends. It was pure magic and everything our souls needed.

Now, with a gigantic plastic ball booming toward me, I needed to figure out how to stop it. In that moment, I had an idea. I made myself as big and wide as I could. My arms were stretched out to the max, and I was in a light sumo squat, feet firmly planted onto the ground.

I remember the ball smooshing into me without knocking me over; I was able to recover quickly, and I was off! Pushing the ball with my hands and running as fast as my legs would go. Before I knew it, I made it to the other side, and Kyle was alongside me, pushing it together, back in the other direction. We crossed the finish line completely spent, knowing we left it all on that field.

If you want a laugh and to see what the competition is all about, we have a video on our YouTube channel *Being Bethunes*, documenting our entire experience, even meeting Dolly.

The entire competition went by in a blur, yet I still can sit and savor in the moments of it.

Have you ever been so grateful for an experience that your gratitude spilled out in the form of tears?

For this challenge, I wanted to focus on giving gratitude for everything in my life right then. I've been doing this to change my mindset and flush out the day-to-day negativity; I thought I'd continue doing it at the challenge too.

When you can experience negativity and be able to allow yourself to feel and then release it, you're able to stay in a centered mindset. You're observing your situation from a new perspective rather than inserting yourself into it and falling into the cycle of worry and fear.

I kept that gratitude mindset all week long.

When we were first presented with the opportunity to compete in the family challenge, we were excited. However, we truly didn't realize the experience we were about to have.

Transformative is the only adjective that genuinely describes what happened to us in those six days.

I witnessed my son and my partner completely come out of their shells and do things they would've NEVER done. Kyle said one of those things was his FAVORITE part of the challenge.

Not only did we strengthen our communication and ability to work together as a team, but we grew as individuals too.

I have so much gratitude for Jess, Ben, Nicole, the other families, and the entire crew. Every single person we met and interacted with was an absolutely delightful human being. Core memories were made that we will carry with us for the rest of our lives.

If you get a chance to do something out of the ordinary, DO IT. Life is a big adventure, and in order to grow and live it to the fullest, you have to step outside of your comfort zone. The only things in life you'll regret are the chances you didn't take.

Take the trip. Go on a hike. Ride the coaster. Go skydiving. Do the thing that scares you. When you get uncomfortable and take those chances, you discover more about yourself than you ever would have before.

With each challenge we completed we learned something about ourselves and each other. We worked together as a team, and we were able to have clear communication the whole time.

We had minimal disruptions and no name calling. We'd all been supportive and encouraging to each other. It looks like the time in Bodhi surely paid off; we were using all of the tools we'd learned in the last few years, and I couldn't have been prouder.

We had to come back to film the finale of the show in November of 2023. Currently we were in Beattyville, Kentucky camping at our friends' RV park, Firefly Hills. Our friends Tonja and Troy graciously allowed us to leave Blue Betty at the campground while we boarded our dogs and drove our van back down the 300 miles to Pigeon Forge, Tennessee.

I remember being a young girl and watching the *Beverly Hillbillies* movie with Jim Varney. In one magical scene, Dolly Parton was acting as herself and wearing a shiny diamond crystal-emblazoned mini gown and singing "Happy Birthday" to Jed Clampett on stage. From the moment she walked out, glimmering in ethereal splendor, with the voice of an angel, I thought she was just the coolest human being ever.

Throughout the years, my love for her only grew. She was a beautiful human, an amazing advocate for literacy, and has always been true and authentic to herself. Truth be told, she exemplified a lot of what I needed as a child and didn't get.

Oddly enough, as a little girl, I'd always had this feeling I would meet her one day.

That day was now here.

As I am dressed in a highlighter yellow family challenge shirt, black stovepipe jeans, with an aqua blue shaved head and my knitted crocheted vest, my palms are sweaty thinking about meeting this person I've never met but have always admired.

Would she be the same person I'd always hoped she was? I was about to find out....

The crew opened the doors and ushered our family in. I could hear this Southern, bold, and familiar voice call out, "You must be the BETHuuuNE family!"

When Dolly came into view, she was that same glowing ethereal angel she had been decades ago whom I admired from a movie. Her smile was radiant, and her energy so pure and loving. With Dolly in the room, she just makes you feel like you're home in your most comfortable PJs, drinking an earl grey tea, listening to the rain hit the tin roof.

Dolly hospitably motioned for us to sit and begins to chat with us about the challenge. Joking with the kids, asking about gobbling up the pancakes. She teased about being able to get us into Dollywood and then asks if there's anything else we would like her to know....

Yes. Yes, I absolutely poured my heart out to Dolly Parton and professed my nearly lifelong admiration for her being such a good human being and role model for so many, myself included.

She smiled and gave genuine gratitude for my compliment, and my heart was so full. I got to feel seen, valid, and heard by Dolly Parton. What an extraordinary memory that will always be.

Shortly after our quick conversation and all the families had their turn privately, we all got to come back in, and I took a SELFIE with Dolly, and she hugged me so tight. Her energy is everything I hoped it would be.

We said our goodbyes, and it really left me reflecting on my childhood and how I was raised. Just because my mom couldn't show me the things I wanted in my life didn't mean there weren't others who were there, modeling them for so many people. To me, one of my role models was Dolly, showing me that being kind to everyone was possible because she does it every day. I can say that now from personal experience.

Someone who inspires many people doesn't always have to be someone famous. It can be a teacher, a coach, an aunt, a postal worker. There are so many good people all over this planet from whom we can learn and grow. We simply need to take the time to observe the people around us and how they make us feel. If they have a trait that you love, you can merge it onto your own highway to happy and incorporate it into who you want to evolve to be.

NOMAD NO MORE?

We did something that I never thought we'd do after being on the bus for nearly five years.

In November of 2023, we completed our family challenge and met my idol. We were currently driving through Georgia on our way to spend winter in central Florida.

Our son Eli wanted us to sit still long enough for him to play a season of soccer, which would be about eight weeks. The longest we like to be anywhere is for about a week, and we were unsure of how this was going to go....

After much deliberation with the family and wanting to make sure each of our needs are seen, validated, and heard, we made the decision to get what they call a "seasonal site" for three months. By doing this, we wouldn't have to move, and Eli could play soccer. The sites required a minimum of twelve weeks to get the seasonal discount, so we figured we would make the best of it and spend the holidays with and around family.

Kyle was thrilled to get to play pickleball every day too. Molly was over the moon to spend every single day with her friends, and Ben was stoked to have great internet for gaming. As for me, I was sitting there terrified.

While we were driving through Georgia, we got into a bus accident. Luckily, everyone was fine, and our bus suffered only minor damage. The other car was totaled, but the driver was alive and unhurt. However, the accident cracked open my PTSD from the accident in which we lost our son Ethan. Now, being in a bus accident was a reality for me, and I was now utterly terrified about going back to stay in central Florida, where our original accident happened.

As we were pulling into that central Florida campground, I wasn't feeling well at all. I had a high fever, I was extremely lethargic, and my entire body felt like it was whacked repeatedly with a sack of potatoes. This went on for pretty much all of December, and I was grateful that I felt better just in time for Christmas.

Truth be told, my body needed rest. Usually, I don't listen, and I have to get very sick for my body to be able to get what it needs from me. After having this nasty virus for almost a month, I vowed to find balance in listening to what my body needs when it first needs it.

Our winter had a rough start, and with the property sold a few months earlier, we wanted to take the kids on an actual vacation and have some fun! There was an upcoming cruise with our membership group, Fulltime Families, and we decided to book it at the last minute.

I couldn't have done this without my dog.

I have PTSD, and I get overwhelmed easily. The overwhelm leads to anxiety. The anxiety leads to panic. The panic puts me on the floor, gasping for air.

My PTSD had been increasing since we were in the bus accident back in late November of 2023. Ever since, I'd been having random panic attacks that come out of the middle of nowhere.

Since I get overwhelmed very easily and driving is a massive trigger, there are not many places I go without Kyle driving. Even in public, if it's a super crowded space, my airway starts to constrict, and panic ensues.

It was hard to be in Florida that winter. It's where all of my trauma comes from. Being here and staying a short distance away from the interstate where Ethan was killed had been devastatingly difficult for me.

When we learned about the opportunity to take a cruise, we thought it would be fun! Sailing the seas with some of our best friends, having a blast? Yes, please! We had been on eleven previous cruises when we lived a traditional life. It was how we vacationed, and we loved it!

Little did we know we'd be detouring off our highway to happy and merging into finding balance on the water!

Now though, this meant leaving on a designated trip from our home on wheels. We'd never done that before, and it was a massive trigger for me. We were going on vacation when Ethan was killed. Every time we get packed up to leave as a family in the car, I'm terrified that there could be a chance we won't all be coming back. This cruise would be a big deal for me.

We tossed around the idea of bringing Theodore and what that would look like. It was a big list to outweigh the pros and cons of bringing a service dog on a cruise. Bottom line, it wasn't going to be easy, and it would add some major challenges.

Having Theodore work for me while we are in our bus or the surrounding area isn't too difficult on him. He can come home, take his vest off, and be a dog. But a seven-day cruise, surrounded by water (which Theodore is not a huge fan of by the way) with no real grass, trees, or fire hydrants to go potty on? Not to mention all the attention you get from going on a cruise with a service dog. Dogs aren't usually on cruises, and we knew that it might make things even more stressful.

When you multiply that with him not having an area to run around or exercise in and being confined to a ship, without being able to leave when you want, had us very concerned.

Kyle and the boys were totally okay with Theodore coming; in fact, they were elated! Sometimes Eli uses Theodore to calm him down and level out his big emotions. We knew it would be great to have Theodore with us, just for that. The problem, however, was with Molly.

She was worried Theodore would take away from her cruise experience because I wouldn't be able to do anything fun. I felt so much guilt for my PTSD, and I didn't want it to ruin everyone's trip. So, I made the decision to leave Theodore at home.

Shortly after I told Kyle that we'd be leaving him behind, Carnival Cruise Lines gave us a call, reminding us that they needed us to send his vaccines over, so he could go.

I took that as a sign from the Universe that Theodore absolutely needed to be on this cruise with us. I'm big on signs and following them. They lead you to where you're meant to be, to your purpose in this life. I quickly sent the vaccines in, and it was decided.

On the second day of the cruise, Kyle's depression knocked him off his feet while I'd been just finding balance and getting my sea legs. Granted, Theodore was having trouble going pee on the ship, so I had to manually express his bladder in our stateroom shower, and still I was surprisingly okay.

Kyle, however, was not. There were many times he never left the stateroom. He was not only depressed, but also seasick as well. Most days, Theodore lay with Kyle, and I was able to get some alone time walking the ship while the kids went off with their friends.

The rest of the cruise was, in retrospect, kind of a disaster. I was having panic attacks left and right, the cruise line was unequipped to accommodate someone with an invisible disability, and Kyle was sinking to his lowest he'd ever been.

With all of that going on, I was rightfully nervous to take Theodore off the boat into another country; we'd never done it before, and we surely didn't know if it would be wise with my PTSD being triggered several times a day.

The vaccines were also an issue for me. Jamaica and Grand Cayman required extra vaccines and testing for him to get, above and beyond what he already had. I felt like it wasn't worth over inoculating him just so we could go into a country for the day.

We still hadn't heard back from Mexico about whether his current vaccines and testing would be accepted. I had made peace with the fact I'd more than likely be staying on the boat the entire cruise. It's okay; I knew it was best for Theodore, and I didn't want to be selfish when he was already going to be working so hard for me this week.

Each morning in port, they would call my stateroom before disembarking and let me know if the country would let Theodore in.

The call came in for Jamaica. "Sorry, ma'am, they won't be allowing you in; you'll have to stay on the ship."

These calls were just reminders; I knew they wouldn't be accepting us.

Next port, Grand Cayman, same sentiments.

I was expecting Cozumel to be the same story. We'd been to all these places before several times, so we all weren't too upset about having to stay on board. We loved the port days because the ship was empty, and we could actually enjoy the amenities not being crowded.

The night before, I got a call to my stateroom. "Mrs. Bethune, Mexico might let your dog in. We will have to wait in the morning for confirmation."

Oh, my word. What?! We might actually get to go ashore?!

I didn't want to get my hopes up, but I also wanted to have an idea of what to do if they said yes.

However, the kids didn't want to get off the boat, and I didn't feel comfortable leaving them onboard so Kyle and I could both go. At the same time, I knew that Theodore would really love to pee and poop on solid ground.

I made up my mind.

If they approved us to go ashore, Theodore and I would be venturing into a foreign country by ourselves. One dog. One human. We were doing this!

The shrill sound of the phone ringing stopped me mid-sentence, and I rushed over to the receiver. The sweet feminine voice on the other end said, "The Mexican authorities want you to meet them in the library on deck five to do their visual inspection. If that passes, he can go to Cozumel."

Holy crap.

I was starting to get nervous, questions in my head swirling. Will he pass? What is the test? How is he going to react? Am I really doing this? Will I panic? How can I navigate a foreign country alone—I can't even go outside of our campground without being in panic?

I took a deep breath and made my first step to the door, Theodore in tow. If I didn't go now, I would sink back into fear and stay on the ship.

As it turns out, the test was simple. They had to look at his teeth, ears, sanitary area, and observe his behavior. He passed with flying colors! I got the go ahead to meander around the island with my service dog!

As Theodore and I bounced down the gangway, I felt my familiar yellow feeling. My knowing. The nudge that keeps me safe. It was here with me, and it felt warm and familiar.

Look out world! I've got my service dog and all the good feels—here we come!

Of course, we got points and stares, mainly people totally shocked to see a big fluffy poodle walking through the markets at the port. Mostly though, it was the locals saying how beautiful Theodore and I were. I understand only very limited Spanish, but I knew what they were saying.

Theodore was just elated to not be on that boat anymore, and I was truly enjoying being out on my own like I used to be able to do without difficulty.

We strolled pass the gates of the port and went into the town. The town had a main two-lane road with the ports and water on one side and little businesses and restaurants on the other.

I went straight across the crosswalk and veered to the right. It didn't really feel right, but I felt the need to keep going.

I passed by each shop filled with dreamcatchers, coconut carvings, shot glasses, and many other trinkets to take home. I was getting more and more confident on my own. I knew that Theodore was with me. He is my safety net, and I know that he's got me.

I always follow that yellow feeling on my serendipitous days, and today was no exception.

All I had was a twenty-dollar bill in cash and my debit card. In all of my excitement to get Theodore off the boat, getting cash at the ATM on board slipped my mind. So that meant I'd need to stay close to town. A taxi ride would be beyond above my budget.

The shops in the direction I was walking were dwindling down, and I felt my yellow nudge tell me to go back the other direction. So, I happily followed.

The great thing about having a service dog is not many people approach you to buy things; they let you walk on by. Theodore wasn't distracted by people stopping to pet him, and I was staying calm.

It was getting toasty as we passed the touristy area, consisting of the Hard Rock Cafe, Señor Frog's, and all the other chain establishments you'd expect. I wasn't really hungry. All I felt was needed was to get to the water, and it wouldn't be long until I would find that in walking distance.

I crossed the road to get to the other side, and as my feet made it to the sidewalk, something up ahead caught my gaze.

The sidewalk I was on had about a two-foot solid white painted stone wall to my left, the trees and brush keeping the water completely out of sight, and the bustling town street to my right.

As my vision came into focus, I saw a middle-aged couple in their mid to late fifties looking at an opening in the wall. The trees were really overgrown, making it hard to see anything beyond the wall.

The couple chose to turn away from the opening and walk back in the other direction.

My curiosity was piqued. My anticipation was mounting… what was down here?

After a thirty second speed walk, Theodore and I made it to the wall opening, and what I saw shocked me. There was an old stone staircase, leading down into a completely overgrown cove. My knowing guided me down the stairs.

Without hesitation, Theodore and I both were bounding down the stairs, full of adventurous wonder.

By the time I got down to the last step, I noticed an abandoned cement pavilion to my left. I assumed a diving charter or restaurant that must have closed down years before. As I glanced to the left, I saw a wooded alcove, teeming with birds and wildlife.

When I finally focused on what was ahead of me, I was amazed!

It was a rocky beach! Nobody else was here—just me, Theodore, and the Caribbean Sea.

I set down my bag and pulled out Theodore's collapsible bowl for water. He happily lapped up every last drop.

While he was getting hydrated, I took a few steps closer to the jagged shoreline.

It was a totally breathtaking view.

Wearing my Earth Runners, I stepped out onto a rock, Theodore standing safely behind. I found my physical balance and drew my attention to my breath, admiring the crashing waves against the shore. I looked up to the clouds, balancing my mind by gazing up at their shapes as they floated out of view.

I had made it. Theodore and I made it to this beautiful private paradise, to a completely different country! Not only did I accomplish that, but I also did it while staying balanced and calm.

This is what freedom felt like, and it felt goooood.

I knew, if I could use nature to find balance in that week of PTSD hell, I could find balance anywhere there's nature.

To this day, Kyle is still growing through what he experienced during that cruise. It was a major part of his healing journey, and truthfully, mine too.

✋ REST STOP #4
BALANCE YOUR MIND

Seven words kept coming up for me in 2023 that I knew I'd need to use to grow through in 2024 were:

Find nature. Discover yourself. Heal your soul.

Over and over and over and over. I started paying attention to them as soon as they popped up. I'd typically feel them when I had my hands full, unable to understand what they meant, so I'd take a mental note to process it later.

The year 2024 was all about using nature to realize how far I've grown in mind, body, and soul. If you learn balance, you live in harmony.

I spent a lot of time out in nature last year on many types of terrain. Not only did I need physical balance to hop on the rocks or swish through water, I also found I had to have mental balance too.

For me, it began with adjusting my mindset. I put thought into my words that I used not only to others, but to myself. I pondered how my words would affect whomever I said them to.

I took negative feeling words and went in a positive direction with them.

When I had something I wanted to work on or improve, I evolved it to say, "It's something that I'm learning to have more balance in."

I discovered if it felt more positive, I actually wanted to do it. When it felt more negative, I wanted to run away from it. The same task, just spun with a positive mindset.

I started to be more balanced in criticism of myself and the criticism I spoke to others. When I started being impeccable with my words in the way that my internal voice spoke to me, the words I spoke to others were just as happy as I was on the inside. My words to others were absolutely a reflection of how I felt on the inside about myself.

The tool I've used the most among all other tools I have in my emotional management toolbox?

Going on a walk each day.

Yes, you're reading that right. It all started with going on a walk each day. When I went on a walk, not only was I strengthening my balance physically, I was also finding balance in getting to know myself mentally by having to sit in my own head and wait for answers to come to me.

How it works:

At a time during the day that you have a little ten-minute window, go for a walk. Put your phone on do not disturb and go walk outside of your building, in the park, even right out into your backyard. Admire all the little things around you, starting with the nearest tree. Look at the little veins in each leaf and the kind of bark that's covering the trunk. When you're ready to move on, walk slowly until you notice what else seems ordinary. Maybe that could be a really cool black and grey rock with shiny flecks sticking out of the ground. Observe it. Gaze at the pattern and appreciate that is bajillions year old earth, and you get to experience it.

Keep slowly walking, pausing at whatever piques your interest, and at the end of those ten to fifteen minutes, you'll feel so balanced, and you'll have gratitude for the tiniest of things in life. You'll feel your stress levels decrease, and clarity returns to take on your day.

Set a goal at the beginning of your day to go on one ten-minute walk. For me, it's easier to take things day by day rather than to set my expectations and have them disappointed when I don't achieve that lofty goal.

I looked at my day and what I had planned, and I knew what things would cause me to feel very stressed, so I scheduled my walk right after those. I knew to get through my day and after them I'd need a breather. Because I've found balance in my mind, I now can listen to when my body tells me I need a walk, and I take it right then.

After we left Florida in March, my PTSD became more manageable, and Kyle's depression was lifting ever so slightly each day. The farther we drove on the highway away from Florida, the better we felt.

Our goal for heading west this spring was to look for property. We knew we didn't want to stop traveling; we just wanted a place of solace to come back to and plug into that was ours. When you live in campgrounds or on boondocking land, you never really own it. We knew it was time to put down roots out west; we just weren't exactly sure where.

A SHORT AND SQUATTY PINE TREE

I awoke from this startling dream one night in March. I sat straight up in bed, puzzled by what I just experienced.

I was standing in a pasture. In the middle of this pasture was a short and squatty youth pine tree. Behind this unusual tree was a hilly mountain, covered in the same kind of trees. In that moment I felt my nudge go "this is your property," and I woke up calm yet shaken. I didn't think much of it and went about daily life. Honestly, I forgot about it.

Here we were not two months later in Mora, New Mexico. I was standing in a pasture, looking at a squatty pine tree with a hilly mountain of similar trees behind it.

You know in the movies when the camera is in a wide shot of a person, and at the speed of light, zooms in on the person's face and a lightbulb appears over their head as a *ding ding ding* sound rings out? I had that experience at that moment. I instantly went back to my dream and knew this was our property we'd been searching for.

We put in an offer that day, and the sellers accepted. We'd only ever spent four days in Mora, New Mexico before we bought a piece of land. Is that crazy? Absolutely it is. I also know that so many crazy things we have done in life has helped us discover what it means to truly live.

For the past few months, we have lived off-grid on our new property. It has 360-degree mountain views and forty-four acres of land ranging from pasture to high desert to a forested mountain. This spring, I had my own meadow of wildflowers. The property has quartz crystals all over, wild desert sage for clearing, as well as wild asparagus that sprouts up. In early fall, we have our own wild apple trees bearing fruit.

It's too early to truly write about because I'm still feeling through the magic of this land and getting to know our community.

As I sit and reflect on our time here thus far, I realize that I am finding balance anywhere I am. My life began in turmoil with my parents passing their generational trauma down to me, and currently through my life choices, I am on a beautiful piece of magical land living in our bus in New Mexico. Every day I find balance, peace, and contentment.

I began to truly live when I took a huge chance and moved my family into a bus. This life isn't conventional, but it's one where we do and feel our best every single day. We went from living in heavy emotions to now fully experiencing them all while maintaining balance.

I want you to have this life experience too, and it doesn't have to look like living in a bus. You don't have to have all the answers; you just have to do a little bit each day to achieve your dream. Every single day, we chose to do a little something to move into a bus. Every day we chose to show up in our couple, how we refer to our relationship, with the tools we were learning in therapy. In every big moment of our lives, we have made little decisions that have had a positive impact.

I truly believe all of that can be yours if you get to know yourself first by choosing to do one of these things each day. Consistency is the key.

Give gratitude (Page 55)
Seek silence (Page 92)
Observe the Moment (Page 98)
Balance your mind (Page 133)

If I told you that you could have the life of your dreams, and it all began with something free, it would just take fifteen minutes a day to start. Would you do it?

I genuinely believe that if you do these things consistently, you'll be well on your way to merging onto your highway to happy. Something I want you to always remember and hold tight is that happiness isn't about arriving at a destination; it's about finding balance in all your emotions on your journey. When you can do that, you can achieve peace. Peace is a state of being greater than any drug you'll ever experience. Peace means that you are aware that you are in balance of all the things in that very moment, and all's right with the Universe.

Then anxiety comes in, and it's an opportunity to use your tools to find balance again 🫶

💜 jenn

P.S. You are enough, just as you are, right in this very moment.
P.P.S. You've made it through every bad day you've ever had.
P.P.P.S. Trust yourself. Your soul knows the way.
P.P.P.P.S. I love you.
P.P.P.P.P.S. As I am about to send this final copy to the editor, my partner of nearly twenty years asked me for a divorce.

AFTERWORD

On September 16, 2024 my partner of nearly twenty years found himself in the deepest cycle of depression that year since the cruise we took back in February.

This particular day happened to be the thirteenth anniversary of the car accident that killed our son Ethan.

As I do every year, I take that day moment by moment. We had a therapy session earlier in the week to set protocol in place specifically for those few days. Ethan's birthday is three days after the accident, so it's a week full of heavy emotions for me.

I had been feeling great sadness that morning, and the protocol was that Kyle was going to be more attentive in the days leading up, trying to notice when I wasn't okay and giving care in that moment.

Feeling extremely low after just having a flashback of the accident, I came to Kyle for care.

Kyle giving me care is something we have been really focusing on during therapy sessions in the recent year. Unfortunately, when he's in depression, the last thing he has energy for is recognizing my needs.

Me asking for him to give me a little more care that I needed triggered him and set him off. His eyes went dark and soulless. He began to lash out with his words saying things like "we haven't worked for a while," and "it's better if we weren't together; it's been a long time coming. Relationships shouldn't be this hard. We are better off divorced."

I was in utter shock.

Our marriage felt like it was the best it had been in such a long time. He and I had healed an intense amount of trauma together, leading us to open up to each other as far as we'd ever had. So, to hear Kyle yell these things at me, it was coming out of left field.

He was so serious. He wasn't budging. I crumpled to the floor in a heap of tears. Today of all days was the one he did this on....

Kyle got up from laying in our bed, walked past me, grabbed the car keys, and he left without even giving me one notice on the floor.

I knew that wasn't My Kyle. That was Triggered Kyle. Deep down I knew he didn't mean those words, but damn did they cut like a knife. The feeling of betrayal and abandonment washed over me, as much of it did most of my childhood and the majority of mine and Kyle's marriage.

Kyle never really learned he had emotions besides anger and happiness. He was never really equipped with the understanding of women as emotional beings and needing to feel supported by their spouse. Honestly, I hadn't truly begun to learn about emotions until about four years ago myself.

As I am pondering the past eighteen years with Kyle, I am using this current divorce trigger as a mirror, to reflect on our relationship and if I wanted to continue it.

For the majority of the years I've been with Kyle, his triggers happened daily. Me advocating for myself was a guaranteed trigger for him, filled with him gaslighting me, making me believe the entire trigger was my fault. With each trigger, I'd internalize it, and it turned into unhealed trauma of abandonment.

While Kyle was away, the kids and I were together at the bus. They are well-versed in Kyle's triggers, and the four of us jump into protocol as soon as they happen. For the past few years since beginning therapy, we have involved the kids in going and include them in all life decisions to get their perspectives. Kyle's depression and triggers are no different. To coexist in this space, we all have to work together.

Right now, Kyle's depression was working against us, and it was all coming to a crashing halt on my highway to happy.

When I have big overwhelming emotions come in, I like to clean and organize the bus. It gives me something productive to do, so I don't focus on the emotions I am experiencing. Rather, it puts me in a meditative state in a sense, to observe my emotions instead of inserting myself into them.

As I was tidying, my journal fell from the shelf and onto the floor. As I picked it up, the page it landed on was from 2019, the year of marriage hell. In the journal entry, I explained how all I wanted was for Kyle to try. I just wanted him to try for our relationship and grow as a couple together.

This wasn't exactly a journal I wrote in often but every year or so when I had a nudge to document something in it. It was usually events related to self-growth or our marriage. I flipped to the next entry and began to read my curvy writing.

The entry I made about two years later was entirely different than the previous one. It was 2021, and we'd been traveling for a year and a half, right before we had found the footage of Gabby's van. In this writing, I was describing joy and how we had found it as a couple because Kyle suggested joining me in therapy.

In that moment, I realized something.

Kyle had been consciously trying since the day in Acton, California when he asked me if we could go to therapy together. Since then, he went from being depressed for thirty days a month to now maybe having seven to fifteen days of depression. Looking back, I could see the growth of just how far we both have come as not only a couple but as individuals too.

After realizing how much I wanted Kyle to try in my previous journal entry, I made the conscious choice to keep trying with Kyle.

Kyle asking for a divorce led me down a rabbit hole of self-discovery. Probably the most important self-discovery I've done to date. I can't wait to share more of my inner world and life lessons with you, to help you grow in yours, in my next book for you.

ACKNOWLEDGMENTS

There are so many people who have had a hand in helping me navigate life's detours along my highway to happy. The first I want to thank is *you.*

I could do all the things right in the universe, but if you didn't pick up this book and read it, none of them would have mattered. I am genuinely grateful for you, no matter what you may have learned or even if you didn't enjoy the book; I am still grateful you took time from your life to read about mine.

I believe that time is the greatest gift you can give someone. That could be reading a book and also writing it. Thank you for being here with me.

My partner Kyle, you are everything my soul needs to grow and vice versa. The Universe knew what it was doing when it bonded us together, and I have gratitude every day for it.

Ben, Molly, and Eli, you are my heart that walks around outside of my body. Thank you for helping me heal my inner child by allowing me to see life through your eyes. I will be forever in gratitude to each of you for that. For you each helped me heal my soul in your own unique way. I will spend the rest of my life being the mother you deserve, doing my best every single day.

My therapist, Jess. I am forever grateful for you helping me save me. Living in balanced joy feels really damn good. Thank you for being who you are and doing what you do; you save more lives than you'll ever know.

Nichole, I am so sad for the way we were brought together, and I am so grateful that Gabby and Ethan connected us. You will never truly know what going to that lighthouse did for my life. I am so grateful for your friendship and love. To the entire Schmidt/Petito Family: Your resilience and strength is something no one should ever have to endure. I admire, respect, and love you all so very much. You're some of the most beautiful humans I've ever met. Jackie C., the kindness you and Kreg showed me that day lives in my heart forever. I have so much gratitude for you, what you did, and how amazing of a human you are.

Sandy and Jed, I am serious when I say that hug will be one of the best hugs I've ever had when Sandy gave me one after we found the footage. The moments we have shared together, I can't even put into words how life changing that was for me, and I am so grateful you both were there. Not to mention, you two put your lives on hold for nearly two months to help us build a campervan in rural Washington state. I just love you both so very big.

Kyle's parents, who I call Mom and Dad: I am beyond grateful for your love throughout the years. As our family grew, your hearts expanded, loving each and every one of us. I'll never forget that set of tires when Kyle and I first started dating. You and Mom have always just wanted to make sure we have stayed safe on our highway to happy. I love you both so much.

My Robin Bird, you flew into my life when so many things for me were up in the air. Thank you for always being you in every moment you're in, doing exactly what you're meant to do. I am so Jenn-uinely grateful you are in my life and we get to grow together.

Carolynn and Amy, this opportunity to share my stories with the world wouldn't have been possible without you both. There's been so many hard times and disappointments over the last year, yet you both have been right there, pivoting along with me. I am so grateful and think the world of you.

I have always appreciated straight-to-the-point-kind-of people, and it was no surprise that I liked Debby Englander instantly. Thank you for believing in my life so much so that you advocated all the way for me. Also, I'm really grateful you taught me that CAPS doesn't have the impact I thought it did.

I wouldn't be who I am if it weren't for how I was brought up as a child. I want to thank my parents for trying their best that they could in raising me. I know you had your own trauma you were carrying at that time. What I've realized is that you taught me the biggest lesson in forgiveness that I could've ever imagined. I forgive you, and I forgive myself for what was then. In the now, I know we've always been doing our best, conscious or not.

Nan and Uncle Dave, Davie and Kristin: I owe so much gratitude to you for being my blood related family who didn't abandon me over the years. The day after Christmas each year, we gathered at Nan's house, ordering pizza and opening gifts. Those moments are some of the only ones my children got to experience what it was like to be with my side of the family. Thank you for being there for us when everyone else had left. I love you all so very much.

For each of you that were in one of my stories, I genuinely cherish our time together and the impact you've made on my life. Your energy lives in my soul forever, and I can't wait to share space again soon.

To our Skoolie Swarm Family, our Buslife Crew, our full-time family friends, and all of our other fellow nomads; thank you for loving us. I am so grateful for each and every single one of you in the community. You've helped us build a van, been a shoulder to cry on, and helped me grow in ways that I never thought possible. If we have had a conversation, trust me when I say, you've left your energy in my heart. For that, I'm truly grateful.

Jackie, Tabby, Wendy, and Brittany, each of you helped me during times in my life that were dark and bleak. Those times you were there for me, they are ones that alter your soul, and you don't realize it until much later in life—what a huge impact you had on me. I am so grateful for each of you and the memories we have.

To the countless people I've ever had an interaction with, you left energy with me. Either a trigger or a glimmer, and at the end of the day, if you use your triggers to do your shadow work and heal your soul, the triggers are really glimmers after all.

I am most grateful for each of you online or in the physical world that has ever sent me a message, phone call, made a comment, given a like, shot a text to me, an in-person conversation, or any little interaction; I am grateful for you.

You, no matter who you are, how you treat me, or the choices you make, you are a glimmer to me, and I will forever send you genuine love.

ABOUT THE AUTHOR

Jenn Bethune is a nomadic author, happiness coach, and story-teller behind the Jennuinely Being YouTube channel. Living in her bus with her family, she shares in how she found peace and joy after overcoming devastating tragedy.